Parent's Quick Start Guide to Dysgraphia

Parent's Quick Start Guide to Dysgraphia provides parents and caregivers with an immediate overview of dysgraphia and steps they can take to support and encourage their child.

Each chapter is packed with detailed and helpful information, covering identification, strategies for improvement, advocating for your child, and maintaining your child's self-esteem. Summary and resource sections at the end of each chapter give quick guidance to busy readers. Topics include a wealth of research-backed activities, strategies for improving penmanship, making writing fun, technological assistance, and more.

Offering straightforward, easy to understand, and evidence-based information, this book is a go-to resource for caregivers parenting a child with dysgraphia.

James W. Forgan is Associate Professor of Special Education at Florida Atlantic University, USA, where he prepares teachers to educate children with dysgraphia and related disabilities.

Noelle Balsamo is an instructor and consultant specializing in teacher and parent education.

Parent's Quick Start Guide to Dysgraphia

James W. Forgan and Noelle Balsamo
with Katie M. Miller

Routledge
Taylor & Francis Group

NEW YORK AND LONDON

Designed cover image: © Getty Images

First published 2024
by Routledge
605 Third Avenue, New York, NY 10158

and by Routledge
4 Park Square, Milton Park, Abingdon, Oxon OX14 4RN

Routledge is an imprint of the Taylor & Francis Group, an informa business

ISBN: 978-1-032-75407-9 (pbk)
ISBN: 978-1-003-47387-9 (ebk)

DOI: 10.4324/9781003473879

Typeset in Palatino
by Deanta Global Publishing Services, Chennai, India

Dedication

Jim dedicates this book to his dad, Harry W. Forgan, Ph.D.,
an expert writer and the co-author of 12 books for teachers
and parents.

Noelle dedicates this book to her devoted husband and
parenting partner, Frank Balsamo.

Contents

Introduction

There is a general assumption that if your child can read, they can write. Yet, this assumption is false as many children with adequate reading struggle with writing. If you are concerned about your child's writing challenges, you are not alone, and you might have thought, "Could it be a writing learning disability?" Parents like you are often concerned with their child's awful-looking penmanship. Perhaps you noticed your child has an awkward-looking pencil grip. Does your child adequately verbalize thoughts but have significant difficulty putting them onto paper? One young child told his mom it felt like he was having writing wars with his hand. A mom expressed her frustration when she explained her child's writing was so slow and laborious that the writing process was painful for them both. These are all classic warning signs of dysgraphia.

Dysgraphia or written expression difficulty affects from 10% to 30% of kids (Bugday, 2022). Testing for dysgraphia is a process that most kids enjoy. It might involve assessing your child's finger control, as some children can't control their finger movements. A dysgraphia evaluation typically assesses your child's ability to copy from close or farther away. Spelling is assessed. Many times your child's talking ability is compared to his or her writing ability, as many children with dysgraphia are stronger at verbal communication as compared to written communication.

If your child has dysgraphia, he or she might be eligible for classroom accommodations on a 504 Plan. This is the public school document that recognizes your child has dysgraphia and prevents teachers from discriminating against your child's writing. Some children need the accommodation of using technology to help bypass their dysgraphia. Other children need extra time on writing tests. Your child might need a special writing utensil to help correct an awkward pencil grasp.

If your child has weak finger strength, they might need to participate in occupational therapy. An occupational therapist helps develop your child's fine motor skills through activities such as cutting, drawing, or buttoning. You can obtain support from school-based and private practice occupational therapists.

This book provides you with quick, get-to-the-point evidence-based information to help your child. We guide you through the process of identifying dysgraphia, understanding treatments, obtaining accommodations, and supporting your child.

1

Dysgraphia Explained

Feeling like dysgraphia is *"Greek to you"*? You are not alone! Although awareness is increasing, dysgraphia remains a lesser diagnosed and lesser understood learning challenge by parents and educators alike (Kalenjuk et al., 2022). So, let us begin by breaking down this seemingly perplexing term and get straight to the "root" of the problem.

As illustrated in the above graphic, *dysgraphia* is a Greek term in origin, which means, in the simplest terms, a "condition of impaired writing" (International Dyslexia Association [IDA], 2023). For the estimated 10%–30% percent of the population of children identified with the condition (Chung et al., 2020), dysgraphia is a complex neurological condition that makes it difficult for them to translate their thoughts and/or spoken language into writing despite having:

♦ Otherwise, age-appropriate skills.
♦ Average to above-average intelligence.
♦ Exposure to quality writing instruction.

DOI: 10.4324/9781003473879-1

The hallmark of dysgraphia is marked deficits in the "physical act of writing," particularly *handwriting* and *spelling* (McCloskey & Rapp, 2017). However, dysgraphia is also characterized more broadly by persistent impairments in any aspect of the writing process including:

- Transcription (handwriting, typing, spelling).
- Grammar (knowledge of sentence form and structure).
- Written expression (conceptualizing, drafting, revising text-based information).

Coming to Consensus: What Exactly Is Dysgraphia?

The exact definition and criteria for dysgraphia continue to be updated and refined as identification and knowledge increase over time. In the professional literature, there remains some controversy as to what extent two broad skill sets (the physical act of writing vs. cognitive processes involved in expressing oneself in writing) are impacted and how these impairments are best described and measured to determine accurate diagnosis and timely intervention (Chung et al., 2020). One thing all experts in education agree on is… writing is hard! Writing requires a number of physical motor skills and brain functions to work together all at once, including:

- Working memory (ability to mentally retain and manipulate information).
- Spatial perception (making sense of space).
- Orthographic coding (ability to recall and form letters, numbers, etc.).
- Language processing (understanding spoken communication).
- Executive functioning (higher-order cognitive skills related to conceptualization, organization, plan execution, etc.).

In subsequent chapters, we provide a more in-depth explanation of the neurological processes that impact writing ability and provide a better understanding of the complexity of the writing process overall to help you come to terms with how dysgraphia may manifest in your child and, more importantly, what you can do to help. Here, we would like to call your attention to a number of observable characteristics that are common among children with dysgraphia that should not be ignored in the case that your child is in need of assessment and/or more timely intervention (Crouch & Jakubecy, 2007; Richards, 1998).

Common Signs of Dysgraphia

◆ Poor letter formation.
◆ Abnormal size and/or spacing of letters.
◆ Mixture of upper-case and lower-case letters.
◆ Mixture of print and cursive letters.
◆ Frequent spelling errors.
◆ Poor grammar.
◆ Oversimplified sentences.
◆ Lack of capitalization and punctuation.
◆ Poor or awkward pencil grasp.
◆ Difficulty writing in a straight line.
◆ Difficulty following grammar rules in writing but not speaking.
◆ Tires quickly when writing, complains of hand hurting.
◆ Excessive erasing.
◆ Decreased speed in writing.
◆ Decreased speed in copying text.
◆ Overall poor legibility/organization.

Throughout this book, we provide information and resources for parents whose children exhibit some or all of these defining characteristics of children with dysgraphia. We will also help dispel any myths that you may encounter along the way. For now, trust that:

◆ Your child is not lazy!
◆ Your child is not just unmotivated!

- ◆ Your child does not just have messy handwriting!
- ◆ Your child is not just resistant/defiant!

Michelle, the mother of a third-grade son with dysgraphia shares:

> The first time I heard my child had dysgraphia, I was already overwhelmed and then was filled with guilt. All the arguments and ripped up papers at the homework table started to make more sense. My child didn't want to battle with me, he just needed help and I didn't yet know how to give it. I wasn't just bad at helping my child with homework, I just needed to get help to be able to help him. The diagnosis was actually a relief for us both and we understand each other better now.

Kim, the mother of a fifth grader with dysgraphia shares:

> I had never heard the word dysgraphia in my life... if we could go back in time, we would have gotten him tested earlier. We just didn't know it was a thing that could be tested until we found out he had it! Now that we have something to call it, we can talk about it.

No matter where you are on your journey, like Michelle and Kim, you may feel overwhelmed, surprised, or underprepared upon hearing the new term dysgraphia. You may also feel relieved and empowered, and start to see your child's struggles with more clarity knowing this new aspect of how they learn.

In each chapter of this book, we will introduce you to the most up-to-date and relevant research you will need to navigate this diagnosis, make informed decisions, and advocate effectively on behalf of your child. In this first chapter, we will summarize the research by briefly addressing the most frequently asked questions (FAQs) by parents new to this diagnosis to prepare you to delve deeper into what dysgraphia is and what it is not so you can proceed from here with confidence.

What the Research Reports

Is Dysgraphia a Disability? Yes!

Dysgraphia is recognized under the category of a Specific Learning Disorder (SLD). In the American Psychiatric Association's (APA) most recent Diagnostic Statistical Manual of Mental Disorders (DSM-5), a handbook that provides guidelines for clinical diagnosis by physicians, psychologists, and other medical professionals, SLD is defined as a persistent impairment in one or more academic areas: reading, writing, or math (2013). Although the term *dysgraphia* is no longer acknowledged in this most recent updated manual, difficulties with written expression are covered under the umbrella of the SLD label. Dysgraphia is further differentiated into impairments in one or more of the following:

◆ Spelling.
◆ Grammar/punctuation.
◆ Clarity/organization of written expression.

Clinically, SLD is further characterized by the level of support anticipated for each child ranging from mild to severe:

◆ **Mild:** some difficulty with learning but able to compensate with minimal intervention.
◆ **Moderate:** significant difficulties with learning, requiring some specialized intervention.
◆ **Severe:** difficulties with learning, requiring intensive intervention.

Specific Learning Disorder is also an eligible category protected under the Individuals with Disabilities Education Act (IDEA), a federal law that provides guidance to public schools on how to identify and support students who demonstrate persistent learning impairments. If a learning disability is suspected, a comprehensive educational assessment is conducted by a team of school professionals to determine if a child is eligible for special education services. This team will most likely consist of some or all of the following specialists:

- ◆ General Education Teacher.
- ◆ Special Education Teacher.
- ◆ School Psychologist.
- ◆ Occupational Therapist.
- ◆ Speech and Language Pathologist.

Chapter 2 will provide you with a comprehensive overview of how dysgraphia is assessed in clinical vs. educational settings. For now, trust that your child is not lazy or unmotivated. Rather an underlying disability is making the already difficult task of writing much, much harder!

Is Dysgraphia the Same as Dyslexia? No!

Dyslexia and dysgraphia are both learning disabilities, but they are distinct from one another and are diagnosed separately, despite having overlapping characteristics. Dyslexia primarily impacts reading, and dysgraphia primarily impacts writing. It is important to note, however, that the two diagnoses commonly occur together. It is estimated that 30%–40% of children with writing impairments also have difficulty with reading (Chung et al., 2020). Therefore, your child may require further assessment and/or more targeted intervention if impairments are observed in both areas.

Are There Other Disabilities That Commonly Occur with Dyslexia? Yes!

As stated above, writing is a complex skill, and disordered writing is common in children with learning disabilities and/ or developmental delays. Dysgraphia is commonly diagnosed as a secondary challenge for children with attentional deficit hyperactive disorder (ADHD) and children with autism spectrum disorder (ASD), with a reported 90%–98% of children with these diagnoses presenting with co-occurring writing challenges (Chung et al., 2020).

However, an important distinction should be made here. Dysgraphia is NOT on the autism spectrum. Nor is it a form of ADHD. If you are concerned about challenges beyond writing, consult with knowledgeable professionals who can differentiate between common, co-occurring conditions with overlapping criteria and can discuss your concerns more specifically. Here, we focus on how to navigate a dysgraphia diagnosis and how to best support your child in all aspects of the writing process, both mentally and physically.

Is Dysgraphia Related to Intelligence? No!

Dysgraphia is not associated with lower intelligence, and a specific learning disorder can only be diagnosed in a child with average to above-average intelligence (APA, 2013). On the contrary, it is the discrepancy between a child's ability and their achievement in writing that is the hallmark of a learning disorder. We encourage you to help your child understand this difference and will help you boost your child's self-esteem alongside their writing ability in Chapter 10.

Will My Child Grow Out of Dysgraphia? No!

Dysgraphia is a neurological lifelong condition, and taking a "wait and see" approach to writing impairments can greatly inhibit your child's success in school and in a text-rich society as a whole (Kalenjuk et al., 2022). As is true with any learning disability, the earlier the intervention occurs and the more focused the intervention is on the child's core deficits, the better (Grigorenko et al., 2020).

However, no matter what age your child is at the time of diagnosis, a well-developed and specialized educational plan focused on evidenced-based practices will empower both you and your child and set you up for greater success. Chapters 3–8 will provide you with a comprehensive overview of educational interventions that target core deficits of dysgraphia with proven results. From here, we will help you and your child work together smarter not harder… you are both working hard enough!

Quick Start Guide to Supporting Your Child

Don't "Wait and See"

Do the challenges introduced here sound familiar but your child has not yet been diagnosed? If so, your first step is to seek a comprehensive clinical and/or educational evaluation with qualified professionals to determine if your child's struggles are the result of this neurological condition. Start now by reading Chapter 2, and take note of the types of professionals who diagnose in clinical settings and locate providers. Reach out to your child's school and share your concerns to determine if your child is eligible for specialized services under the category of a Specific Learning Disorder. Like Kim, you will want to know sooner than later if dysgraphia is indeed part of your child's learning profile so you can get both of you the help needed. A comprehensive evaluation will also help identify your child's unique set of strengths and deficits. Dysgraphia is not outgrown. Educational interventions are needed and the sooner the better.

Observe and Document

As you can ascertain from the various definitions shared here, there are a number of ways dysgraphia can present at different stages of your child's life and across settings. There are a number of observable signs of dysgraphia such as the ones listed here that can be missed or appear unrelated. Keep in mind that the list provided here identifies common "red flags" associated with dysgraphia but is not an exhaustive list. Not every child who struggles with writing has dysgraphia. Nor will every child with dysgraphia exhibit every sign.

Observe your child's writing behaviors in the home, and take note of what you see to get a better picture of any patterns or frequently occurring struggles. This will help you articulate your concerns more specifically. Keep samples of your child's work, and reference them to help illustrate areas of need and, more importantly, document the progress being made. Although dysgraphia may be new to you, your child is not. You are the number one expert on your child, and feeling prepared with this information will help you continue to be your child's best advocate in this new way.

Take a Team Approach

Like Michelle, you may have been trying to tackle your child's writing struggles on your own before you knew that a learning difference was the root of the problem. Now that you know dysgraphia is a neurological barrier rather than a battle of wills, your next step is to get in touch with the support you need and get your team together. Share this resource with family members who would benefit from knowing more about your child's learning difference. Learn who the school professionals are that your child will be working with, what they do, and how you can work together consistently and effectively as a team. Know what providers are in your community and what clinical services are available to your child. Chapter 9 will help you be a collaborative team member and a knowledgeable advocate to ensure your child's educational needs are being met.

Protect Your Time and Resources

Know what works and what does not. Chapter 3 will help guide you toward evidence-based interventions specific to dysgraphia and help steer you away from unproven, often expensive products or services marketed to parents with children with learning differences. Your child's progress should be closely monitored and transparently reported. Use this resource to be sure the interventions provided and those who provide them are a good fit for you and your child and produce real results.

Ask questions of your providers, ask for data that supports claims made about your child and work samples that illustrate current performance, and document progress along the way. Dysgraphia cannot be cured or outgrown, but science tells us what works. Save your time and resources for scientifically proven interventions and the qualified professionals who provide them!

Summary

As seen in the perspectives shared by the parents here, a dysgraphia diagnosis can come as a surprise even when daily homework battles are the norm. Being a lesser-known learning disorder, a dysgraphia diagnosis label can lead to more questions than answers at first. No, your child is not lazy, messy, or defiant. Your child has a learning difference that significantly impacts their ability to express themselves in writing either legibly or effectively or both. No, you are not at fault for not realizing this sooner. Learning disabilities are what's referred to as hidden disabilities; you can't see it until it becomes a problem, and dysgraphia in particular is not always on a parent's or teacher's radar right away.

This first chapter helps you know what to look for, guides you on what first steps you can take to be sure your child is accurately diagnosed, and provides guidelines for getting the help you both need. The remaining chapters will provide practical strategies to address common challenges encountered in the home and school environments and empower both you and your child to work as a team and with your team.

Resources

Psychiatry.org - What Is Specific Learning Disorder? American Psychological Association (APA)

Dysgraphia: What It Is, Symptoms, Diagnosis & Treatment (clevelandclinic. org) Cleveland Clinic: Dysgraphia

Understanding Dysgraphia - International Dyslexia Association (dyslexiaida.org) International Dyslexia Association (IDA): Understanding Dysgraphia

IDEA Parent Guide - NCLD National Center for Learning Disabilities: IDEA Parent Guide

Dysgraphia vs. Dyslexia: Compare the Differences (understood.org) Understood. Org: Dysgraphia vs. Dyslexia

References

American Psychiatric Association. (2013). *Diagnostic and statistical manual of mental disorders* (5th ed.). https://doi.org/10.1176/appi.books. 9780890425596

Chung, P. J., Patel, D. R., & Nizami, I. (2020). Disorder of written expression and dysgraphia: Definition, diagnosis, and management. *Translational Pediatrics*, *9*(Suppl. 1), S46. https://doi.org/10.21037/tp.2019.11.01

Crouch, A. L., & Jakubecy, J. J. (2007). Dysgraphia: How it affects a student's performance and what can be done about it. *Teaching Exceptional Children Plus*, *3*(3), n3.

Grigorenko, E. L., Compton, D. L., Fuchs, L. S., Wagner, R. K., Willcutt, E. G., & Fletcher, J. M. (2020). Understanding, educating, and supporting children with specific learning disabilities: 50 years of science and practice. *American Psychologist*, *75*(1), 37.

Kalenjuk, E., Laletas, S., Subban, P., & Wilson, S. (2022). A scoping review to map research on children with dysgraphia, their Carers, and educators. *Australian Journal of Learning Difficulties*, *27*(1), 19–63.

McCloskey, M., & Rapp, B. (2017). Developmental dysgraphia: An overview and framework for research. *Developmental Dysgraphia*, 1–18. https://doi.org/10.1080/02643294.2017.1369016

Richards, R. G. (1998). *The writing dilemma: Understanding dysgraphia*. Richards Educational Therapy (RET). 190 E. Big Springs Rd., 92507–4835. Center Press.

2

Assessing for Dysgraphia

Assessing for Dysgraphia Explained

As an informed parent, you want to know your child's specific struggle so you can take action to help. A thorough assessment for dysgraphia can confirm if your child has dysgraphia. So how do you locate a person to assess your child? Various professionals assess for dysgraphia, including occupational therapists, clinical psychologists, school psychologists, and neuropsychologists. While many professionals can assess, there is no stand-alone or sole definitive test or even a standard battery of tests to use to diagnose dysgraphia. Thus, methods for assessing for dysgraphia vary. Furthermore, an occupational therapist might only assess for dysgraphia, whereas a psychologist might assess your

TABLE 2.1 Professionals Evaluating for Dysgraphia

Professional	Type of Evaluation
Occupational Therapist	Fine motor problems, appropriate posture, sensory problems, coordination problems
Physical Therapist	Gross motor and coordination problems
School Psychologist, Clinical Psychologist, and Neuropsychologist	Depending on their experience and training: learning disabilities including dysgraphia, dyslexia, dyscalculia, ADHD, autism, and other related disabilities

DOI: 10.4324/9781003473879-2

child for dysgraphia as one part of a larger evaluation process. Some professionals assess for dysgraphia, dyslexia, and dyscalculia (math) learning disabilities at the same time.

Children use many cognitive systems when writing including:

◆ Critical thinking.
◆ Self-talk.
◆ Memory.
◆ Attention.
◆ Organization.
◆ Sequencing.
◆ Visual-spatial thinking.
◆ Eye-hand coordination.
◆ Fine motor coordination.
◆ Processing speed.

Since many cognitive areas are involved in writing, the examiner must complete a broad assessment that encompasses most, if not all, of these areas. The examiner must rule out specific areas as the cause to identify the specific weaknesses. This helps guide treatment. Sierra was ready to start occupational therapy with her seven-year-old son, but a thorough evaluation identified his fine motor was not the root problem. Her son's difficulty was in sequential memory, so treatment was targeted at helping the child understand sequencing and strengthening his memory. He was putting so much effort into writing that he would forget what he wanted to write. An educational specialist taught him how to use a graphic organizer and outline of key words so he could remember better.

The following are broad cognitive areas an examiner might assess to evaluate for dysgraphia and learning disabilities. Each area is followed by possible tests the examiner might use.

Writing
Woodcock Johnson Tests of Achievement subtests Writing Samples, Spelling, and Sentence Writing Fluency
Wechsler Individual Achievement Tests subtests Alphabet Writing Fluency, Sentence Composition, and Spelling

Kaufman Individual Achievement Tests subtests Written
Expression and Spelling
Tests of Written Language

Phonological Awareness
Comprehensive Test of Phonological Processing
NEPSY II subtest Phonological Processing
Woodcock Johnson Tests of Cognitive Abilities subtest
Phonological Processing

Visual-Spatial Thinking
Wechsler Intelligence Scale for Children subtests Visual Puzzles
and Block Design
NEPSY subtests Arrows, Geometric Puzzles, Block Construction
Woodcock Johnson Tests of Cognitive Abilities subtest
Visualization and Picture Recognition

Visual Motor Integration
NEPSY II Design Copying
Berry-Buktenica Developmental Test of Visual Motor Integration
Bender Gestalt II

Finger Control
NEPSY II Fingertip Tapping

Intelligence
Wechsler Intelligence Scale for Children
Differential Ability Scales
Reynolds Intellectual Assessment Scales

Working Memory
Wide Range Assessment of Memory and Learning
Wechsler Intelligence Scale for Children Working Memory Index
Reynolds Intellectual Assessment Scales Working Memory Index

Executive Functioning
NEPSY II
Delis-Kaplan Executive Functioning System
Behavior Rating Inventory of Executive Function (BRIEF)

Retrieval Fluency
NEPSY II subtest Word Generation

Delis-Kaplan Executive Functioning System subtest Verbal Fluency

Woodcock Johnson Tests of Oral Language subtests Retrieval Fluency and Rapid Picture Naming

Comprehensive Test of Phonological Processing subtests Rapid Number Naming and Rapid Letter Naming

In addition to the above tests, an occupational therapist's evaluation might also include:

- ◆ Assessment of sitting posture.
- ◆ Endurance to maintain whole body attention at the table.
- ◆ Assessment of child's fine motor and in-hand manipulation skills.
- ◆ Ocular motor screening.
- ◆ Assessment of visual motor integration skills.
- ◆ Assessment of pencil grip and paper placement.
- ◆ Observation of the use of the non-dominant or helper hand.

If your child attends a public school, you can make a request for the school psychologist to test your child for dysgraphia. As discussed in Chapter 1, dysgraphia is also called a Disorder of Written Expression or a Specific Learning Disability in writing, depending on which diagnostic criteria is used. Thus, you can request an evaluation for any of these three areas: dysgraphia, Disorder of Written Expression, or a Specific Learning Disability in writing. Provide a document describing the dysgraphia warning signs you observe as well as samples from any of the "do-it-yourself" informal screening assessments described in the Quick Start section on the following pages.

If your child attends a private school, you can bring your concerns to school staff to ask about any available evaluation resources. Many private schools have contracted occupational therapists or psychologists that you can consult with about your concerns. If the school does not have any contractors, they might give you a list of reputable professionals who can provide a private dysgraphia evaluation.

What the Research Reports

There are various theories about how cognitive systems contribute to a person's writing ability. Flower and Hayes (1981) explain the writing process as having three levels. First, the child must conceptualize the idea as a preverbal message held in memory. Second, the conceptualized message is verbalized and the child includes grammatical properties such as correct grammar and spelling. Third, the verbal message is converted into a sequence of motor movements and the written form is created.

Feder and Majnemer (2007) included two components of the writing process: motor and perceptual. The motor component involves fine motor control of the hand to hold the pencil and form letters. The perceptual component includes the person's sensory modalities to maintain attention and use visual perception while writing. The two components work together as visual motor integration or the coordination of the individual's ability to see information and reproduce it in written form.

Other researchers' contributions to understanding writing difficulty include a person's working memory. This is a person's ability to hold information in memory while changing it, such as doing mental math. Working memory in writing is the child's ability to suspend their thoughts and ideas in memory while also recalling spelling and grammatical rules. Beringer and Amtmann (2003) noted the importance of working memory in writing and how it was linked to a person's long-term memory.

Some researchers have begun studying how technology can be used to diagnose dysgraphia. Raza and colleagues (2017) created a white paper mobile application using handwriting technology in which children write on a screen, and the technology is analyzed to use in determining dysgraphia.

Researchers Safarova et al. (2021) have attempted to use digitizing tablets and a pen to study the child's pressure, altitude, and azimuth of the writing pen. Usually, children with dysgraphia place excessive pressure when using a writing instrument. The altitude determines the angle between the surface and the pen and ranges from 0 degrees when lying flat on the device to 90 degrees when the pen is perpendicular to the device. The azimuth parameter specifies the position of the pen on the circle. The researchers noted it is problematic to create a graphomotor abilities rating scale to diagnose dysgraphia, as "Worldwide methods for measuring problems with handwriting are product-oriented and do not have sufficiently established psychometric characteristics or follow old norms and standardizations (p. 153)." Technology will continue to evolve and improve, but at this point in time, a battery of tests appears the best way to diagnose dysgraphia.

Researchers have also studied a child's pencil grasp. The traditional writing grasp, the dynamic tripod, is still thought of as the optimal grasp for handwriting (Graham et al., 2008). Researcher Heidi Schwellnus (2012) also reported three other mature pencil grasps that are functional for children to use. These comprise the lateral tripod, the dynamic quadrupod, and the lateral quadrupod. She concluded that if a child uses one of these four grasps, rather than focusing on trying to change the grasp, a professional's intervention should focus on increasing writing speed and letter formation.

Safarova and colleagues noted, "If the position of the pen during writing is correct, the thumb and middle finger are used for creating the fine-motor movements and the index finger is used for stabilization" (p. 153). So how important is a child's pencil grasp? When assessing a child's pencil grasp, there are two questions to consider.

- ◆ First, does the child hold the pencil in a manner that severely affects their range of movement?
- ◆ Second, is the child using larger muscles to move the pencil instead of their fingers and thumb in unison?

If the answer to either of these questions is "yes," it is appropriate to work on changing the child's grasp before fourth grade.

Quick Start Guide to Assessing for Dysgraphia

Your intuition has told you it might be dysgraphia, and you read the dysgraphia warning signs in Chapter 1. Now you can try some informal and at-home, "do-it-yourself" types of screening assessments to further your insight that your child's struggle could be dysgraphia. Record your concerns in Table 2.2.

Below are seven home-based activities to screen your child for possible dysgraphia.

1. **Strong verbal communication.** In many children, there is a disruption between their ideas and the ability to express them through writing. Think about your child. Does your child speak better than he or she writes? If yes, this supports possible dysgraphia.
2. **Examine the pencil grasp.** Ask your child to hold a pencil and write his or her name. As he or she writes, examine your child's pencil grasp. Is it a typical tripod pencil grasp with the pencil held between the thumb and middle finger with the index finger supporting the pencil? Or is the grasp atypical looking with the thumb wrapped over the index finger? An atypical pencil grasp is a dysgraphia warning sign.
3. **Copy close activity.** This simulates the school task of your child copying from a book onto a piece of paper. On a piece of paper, draw or use the SmartArt feature in Microsoft Word to insert various shapes that start easy to copy and get harder, such as those below. Give your child a pencil without an eraser and ask your child to copy the shape exactly as it appears in the box below the shape.

Your child gets one try with no erasing or turning the paper sideways. How did your child do with this task? This assessed your child's eye-hand coordination which educators term visual and motor integration.

4. **Far copy activity.** This simulates your child copying information from the board while seated at a desk. Use your word processing program and Comic Sans MS font size 96 and

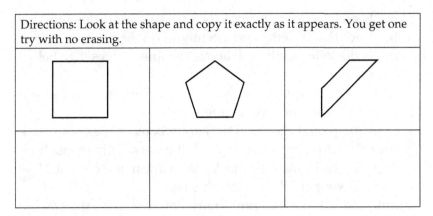

Directions: Look at the shape and copy it exactly as it appears. You get one try with no erasing.

FIGURE 2.1 Close Copy Activity

type these sentences: Boys and girls like to play fun games on Saturday. It can make a bad day feel good. The weekend goes too fast.

   a. Print it out and tape the pages together to make it look like a poster.

   b. Hang this on the wall.

   c. Now seat your child at a table about 10 feet away from the poster.

   d. Read it together and clarify any words your child did not know.

   e. Ask your child to copy this down exactly as it appears.

   f. Once copied, remove the poster from the wall and put it out of sight.

   g. Ask your child to read his or her writing to you.

Observe several things such as: did your child copy this perfectly or were there reversals and misspellings? Could your child re-read their own handwriting? Was this a long and laborious task for your child? Place a mark in Table 2.2.

5. **Examine a writing sample.** Ask your child to write three sentences about things they like to do. Look at your child's writing sample. Pick out a letter that is frequently used in writing such as the letter "a." Find all the "a" letters in the writing sample and compare them to each other. Ask yourself:

  a. Is each "a" letter formed the same way or differently?
  b. Does the "a" letter consistently sit on the line?
  c. Is the letter made well above the line or does it go below the line?

  Draw conclusions, as children with dysgraphia consistently form the same letter differently.

6. **Examine pencil control.** Purchase a book of mazes and ask your child to draw a line through the track without touching the sides. Performing this task shows fine motor control. How well did your child complete this task?

7. **Ask about hand fatigue.** Many children with dysgraphia experience hand fatigue when writing. Ask your child if his or her hand gets tired or feels cramped when writing. Record your opinion below.

Review your responses from Table 2.2. If you checked off three or more, consider obtaining a formal dysgraphia assessment. Bring this book to your appointment or take a picture of the table to use to share your specific concerns. Use this specific information to start the assessment process. Help awaits.

TABLE 2.2 Dysgraphia Concerns Checklist

Informal Dysgraphia Assessment	*No Concern*	*Yes Concern*
1. Does your child perform better when speaking ideas and thoughts as compared to writing them?		
2. Is your child using a standard tripod pencil grasp?		
3. Did your child have difficulty copying shapes?		
4. Did your child have difficulty copying from far away?		
5. Looking at a writing sample, did your child form the letter consistently in the same manner?		
6. Was your child able to maintain pencil control to draw through a maze without touching the side lines?		
7. Does your child's hand fatigue when writing for long periods?		

Summary

Dysgraphia can be assessed in children as young as at least halfway through kindergarten but it often takes an astute parent to bring specific concerns to the school's attention. It's also helpful for you to quantify your concerns by completing informal screening assessments with your child. This provides data to help validate your intuitive concerns. There are occupational therapists, psychologists, and educational specialists waiting to help your child.

Resources

www.Amazon.com: Maze books for kids
www.Amazon.com: Shape tracing and practice workbooks
www.theottoolbox.com: Occupational Therapy Information

References

Berninger, V. W., & Amtmann, D. (2003). Preventing written expression disabilities through early and continuing assessment and intervention for handwriting and/or spelling problems: Research into practice. In H. L. Swanson, K. R. Harris, & S. Graham (Eds.), *Handbook of learning disabilities* (pp. 345–363). Guilford Press.

Feder, K. P., & Majnemer, A. (2007). Handwriting development, competency, and intervention. *Developmental Medicine & Child Neurology, 49*(4), 312–317.

Flower, L., & Hayes, J. R. (1981). A cognitive process theory of writing. *College Composition and Communication, 32*(4), 365–387.

Graham, S., Harris, K. R., Mason, L., Fink-Chorzempa, B., Moran, S., & Saddler, B. (2008). How do primary grade teachers teach handwriting? A national survey. *Reading and Writing, 21*(1), 49–69.

Medwell, J., Strand, S., & Wray, D. (2009). The links between handwriting and composing for Y6 children. *Cambridge Journal of Education, 39*(3), 329–344.

Raza, T. F., Arif, H., Darvagheh, S. H., & Hajjdiab, H. (2017, February). Interactive mobile application for testing children with dysgraphia. In *Proceedings of the 9th international conference on machine learning and computing* (pp. 432–436).

Šafárová, K., Mekyska, J., & Zvončák, V. (2021). Developmental dysgraphia: A new approach to diagnosis. *The International Journal of Assessment and Evaluation, 28*(1), 143.

Schwellnus, H. D. (2012). *Pencil grasp pattern: How critical is it to functional handwriting?* University of Toronto (Canada).

3

Treating Dysgraphia

If you read Chapters 1 and 2, you understand what dysgraphia is and how to assess a child for dysgraphia. Now the important part: how to treat a child's dysgraphia. This chapter explains different approaches for treating dysgraphia, and the following chapters provide even more detailed activities and information.

When your child writes, it can be a mentally overwhelming, physically exhausting, and time-consuming process, so it is no surprise your child might have a negative attitude toward writing. After all, most people avoid difficult tasks that take a tremendous amount of preparation and mental effort. We encourage you to try and be understanding when your child avoids writing or puts forth minimal effort. Your child is not trying to be difficult on purpose; your child has dysgraphia.

Furthermore, it can perplex you and teachers when your child with dysgraphia speaks more eloquently than they can write. For example, one author's child had dysgraphia. The second-grade schoolteacher required weekly homework to write each spelling word in a sentence. Dysgraphia impeded the child's handwriting and ability to put thoughts onto paper so rather than elaborate sentences, the child wrote simple sentences. For the word, "supper," the child wrote, "I eat supper." This simple sentence pattern was repeated for words such as "color" and "inside" with sentences such as "I like to color" and "I go inside." Although the sentences correctly used the spelling word, the teacher did

DOI: 10.4324/9781003473879-3

not like the simplicity of each sentence and noted this in red ink on the paper. This was not the child being lazy but rather coping with dysgraphia.

The dysgraphia also caused messy-looking penmanship so this child's letters would sit above the line, below the line, and occasionally on the line. She formed the same letter in different ways. This child could not produce consistently nice-looking penmanship, and the teacher penalized her for this.

What the Research Reports

Dysgraphia can be treated but not cured. Since dysgraphia presents in various ways, there is no one universal treatment. As noted by Biotteau and colleagues (2019), "Although there is no gold standard method, several strategies have been investigated and scientifically validated" (p. 1880). These strategies are generally therapy-based or educational supports.

In children who need their handwriting strengthened, therapy-based treatment is often completed with an occupational therapist and includes the child completing exercises focusing on writing loops and bridges from simple to complex. According to Berringer et al. (1997), the most effective way to teach the child is by presenting a model that shows the correct order and the use of guideline direction the pencil should follow for the figure to be copied. This was more effective than showing the child a static model and having them trace it.

Researchers Vinter and Chartrel (2010) showed that five-year-old children performed better when they watched a video of a writer who was writing, rather than just showing the child a static model without any directional indications. The least effective method was having the child trace dots to form the figure. They stated, "Therefore, improvement in performance in a writing task requires a systematic training process and cannot be evoked by general graphic tasks as regularly proposed for preschool children; training is needed at least for a short period of time" (p. 483–484).

Many times a child's atypical pencil grasp is a noticeable warning sign for dysgraphia, but Chu (1997) reported that by itself, an atypical pencil grasp did not necessarily result in handwriting difficulties. Children and adults might alternate grasps to account for finger fatigue. However, when an atypical grasp with or without factors such as eye-hand coordination trouble makes handwriting illegible it causes problems. Researchers Cornhill and Case-Smith (1996) reported that test scores for students with good handwriting were significantly higher than those of students with poor handwriting. A child's illegible handwriting results in a functional limitation which leads to teacher grading bias when written assignments look messy. Illegible handwriting can also interfere with math computations when a child or teacher cannot identify their written numerals.

Kushki et al. (2011) showed that within ten minutes, prolonged writing produced muscle fatigue and writing legibility decreased with time. Fourth graders with dysgraphia also wrote faster in a horizontal direction as compared to a vertical direction which implied they tended to work quickly rather than accurately. This has teaching implications, as assigning longer writing tasks to a child with dysgraphia increases the probability the child will turn in a messier-looking paper.

Given the writing challenges that children with dysgraphia experience, researchers Gillespie and Graham conducted a meta-analysis to identify which treatments most helped children with learning disabilities. They concluded the four most effective treatments included, "strategy instruction, dictation, goal setting, and process writing" (p. 468). Strategy instruction involves explicit instruction in the steps of the writing process, explicit instruction in text structures of various writing genres, and guided feedback during the writing process (Gersten and Baker, 2001). Dictation, or what we now call speech-to-text technology, showed that students with learning disabilities who dictated their compositions showed greater improvements in overall written expression performance than students who wrote by hand exclusively. Goals setting for writing and revising was an effective treatment for students in upper elementary and middle grades. Students who engaged in process writing followed the stages in writing, wrote for authentic purposes, and received direct instruction in writing when needed.

Another effective approach for helping children with dysgraphia as identified by Graham and Perin (2007) in their meta-analysis was a summarization technique. Students in grades five to twelve were explicitly taught how to summarize text they read, which then led to the students' ability to write more concise text. The researchers also noted that using word processing had a positive impact on the quality of students' writing.

Educational research on dysgraphia and writing learning disabilities supports that your child's writing can improve with effective treatments ranging from handwriting instruction, strategy instruction, speech-to-text, and typing. Let's now identify specific programs and activities to help your child.

Quick Start Guide to Treating Dysgraphia

Once you have a confirmed diagnosis that your child has dysgraphia, you can identify your child's specific area of weakness, as primary treatments include working with an occupational therapist, instruction from a specialized teacher, or home-based exercises.

Occupational Therapy

As an astute parent, you have an instinct about the quality of your child's fine motor skills. You might have noticed your child's awkward pencil grasp, difficulty cutting using scissors, problems fastening clothing buttons or snaps, or problems holding shoelaces to tie shoes. These signs support the possibility that your child might need to begin working with an occupational therapist. You can locate a pediatric occupational therapist (OT) and:

◆ Check with your child's school, as many have OTs on staff or as consultants.
◆ Ask your child's pediatrician for a recommendation or referral.

- ◆ Check with the American Occupational Therapy Association https://www.aota.org.
- ◆ Search online at websites such as Healthgrades.com. https://www.healthgrades.com/pediatric-occupational -therapy-directory.

Many OTs use the classic program Handwriting Without Tears, which was created by occupational therapist, Jan Z. Olsen, to use with her son, John. This program has been the popular standard for teaching penmanship to students with handwriting challenges. The program has evolved into Learning Without Tears and now includes kindergarten readiness writing, Keyboarding Without Tears, and uses print and technology-based instruction.

Writing Instruction

Specialized educators and tutors provide writing instruction that may include penmanship but more often involves teaching the child the process of writing, including planning, organizing, writing, revising, and publishing. A classic writing planning tool is the brainstorm. Many children with dysgraphia experience difficulty when it's time to think about what to write. A brainstorm gives your child a place to write any idea that comes to mind. Let's say your elementary student is told to write an essay about animals. Your child might not know if he should discuss land animals, water animals, air animals, herbivores, carnivores, domesticated animals, or desert animals. This tool provides a place to jot down all these ideas to consider.

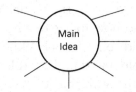

When it is time for the child to plan out their writing, a classic tool is the outline. A tech-savvy approach is using the Inspiration software, which allows your child to brainstorm and outline all within an organized framework. An alternative is using a paper-based square writing format such as the one pictured below.

Your child can follow the format to write a five-sentence paragraph. When it's time to revise, your child can read the piece aloud. Hearing our work helps us proof it. Alternative ways to proof our work are setting the work aside for a day and revisiting it, asking a peer to read and provide feedback, or having an adult review and give suggestions. Some children with dysgraphia find the website Grammarly helps with revising.

Publishing is the fun part of writing. Your child can take his or her rough draft and, if it is not already typed, type it. Other children enjoy using a blank book and writing the piece inside the blank pages. Some children have an approved scribe rewrite the piece. Regardless of the method your child uses to publish the writing, it provides a great sense of accomplishment.

Home-Based Activities

There are many easy-to-use home-based activities to help improve your child's fine motor and writing skills. These include:

Provide opportunities for your child to strengthen finger control by introducing the following activities:

- ◆ Use the classic squeeze grip available online.
- ◆ Show your child how to use one hand's fingertips to take a tennis ball and roll it from his knee up his thigh.
- ◆ Use clay or moldable dough to roll it into a snake. Form the snake into recognizable letters.
- ◆ Use Legos or K'Nex to put pieces together and make fun creations.

Teach your child muscle tension and relaxation. Demonstrate how to clench your fists together and slowly count to five. Then gradually release your fists stretching your fingers outward. Now wiggle your fingers up and down as if you were casting a spell. Next, extend your fingers on your dominant hand. Place your non-dominant hand palm up under your dominant hand and gradually push your fingers upward to stretch them up and slightly backward.

Practice visual motor or eye-hand coordination. Use activities such as:

♦ Play catch together.
♦ Your child can bounce a ball against a wall and catch it.
♦ She can use a pencil and complete a maze or a step-by-step drawing book.
♦ Use a game such as Bop It! to practice listening and completing hand motions under pressure.

Practice writing on the line using raised line paper. This helps kids see and feel the line so their writing does not drift. Practice writing letters using freezer bag writing. You place colored hair gel inside a sealed and taped freezer bag. Your child can place the bag on a hard surface and smooth it out until it is flat. Then use a finger to practice writing words or letters.

At home introduce technology. The Snap Type app was created by an occupational therapist and allows a child to complete any school worksheet on an iPad. Your child takes a picture of a document and then can type responses directly into the worksheet rather than writing it out by hand. Your child can tap on the screen to add a text box or dictate answers, and Snap Type types them on the worksheet.

https://realotsolutions.com/shop/size-matters-handwriting-program/

Another technology is the Dexteria and Dexteria Jr. app to practice fine motor skills. This is available to develop prewriting skills and practice a pincer grip, which can help improve a child's pencil grasp. Learn more at the Apple App Store.

Use Because Neatness Matters. This is an evidence-based and formal remedial handwriting instruction program to help children with dysgraphia and other handwriting struggles. This program was created by an occupational therapist and helps children in kindergarten through second grade learn penmanship. Learn more at becauseneatnessmatters.com

Summary

Although there is no cure for dysgraphia, your child's writing can improve. Treatments include occupational therapy, specialized instruction, and home-based exercises. Technology tools such as speech-to-text or apps such as Snap Type are ways to help your child bypass his or her dysgraphia.

Resources

www.aota.org: American Occupational Therapy Association
www.snaptypeapp.com: Snap Type App
www.lwtears.com/solutions/writing/handwriting-without-tears#idtt: Handwriting Without Tears
www.theottoolbox.com/handwriting: The OT Toolbox
www.inspiration-at.com: Inspiration Software
https://becauseneatnessmatters.com: Because Neatness Matters Hand writing Program
www.realotsolutions.com: Real OT Solutions offers the Size Matters Handwriting Program and other resources to help with cursing and adaptive handwriting

References

Berninger, V. W., Vaughan, K. B., Abbott, R. D., Abbott, S. P., Rogan, L. W., Brooks, A., ... Graham, S. (1997). Treatment of handwriting problems in beginning writers: Transfer from handwriting to composition. *Journal of Educational Psychology, 89*(4), 652.

Biotteau, M., Danna, J., Baudou, É., Puyjarinet, F., Velay, J. L., Albaret, J. M., & Chaix, Y. (2019). Developmental coordination disorder and dysgraphia: Signs and symptoms, diagnosis, and rehabilitation. *Neuropsychiatric Disease and Treatment, 15*, 1873–1885.

Chu, S. (1997). Occupational therapy for children with handwriting difficulties: A framework for evaluation and treatment. *British Journal of Occupational Therapy, 60*(12), 514–520.

Cornhill, H., & Case-Smith, J. (1996). Factors that relate to good and poor handwriting. *American Journal of Occupational Therapy, 50*(9), 732–739.

Gersten, R., & Baker, S. (2001). Teaching expressive writing to students with learning disabilities: A meta-analysis. *The Elementary School Journal, 101*(3), 251–272.

Graham, S., & Perin, D. (2007). A meta-analysis of writing instruction for adolescent students. *Journal of Educational Psychology, 99*(3), 445.

Kushki, A., Schwellnus, H., Ilyas, F., & Chau, T. (2011). Changes in kinetics and kinematics of handwriting during a prolonged writing task in children with and without dysgraphia. *Research in Developmental Disabilities, 32*(3), 1058–1064. http://doi.org/10.1016/j.ridd.2011.01.026

Smits-Engelsman, B., Vincon, S., Blank, R., Quadrado, V. H., Polatajko, H., & Wilson, P. H. (2018). Evaluating the evidence for motor-based interventions in developmental coordination disorder: A systematic review and meta-analysis. *Research in Developmental Disabilities, 74*, 72–102.

Vinter, A., & Chartrel, E. (2010). Effects of different types of learning on handwriting movements in young children. *Learning and Instruction, 20*(6), 476–486.

4

Strategies for Improving Spelling

Spelling Explained

Most people consider spelling an essential skill for academic success since writing is required throughout your child's school years. As former teachers, we've taught spelling using traditional and specialized approaches. Teachers know that repetition helps improve your child's spelling. Thus, elementary school teachers often use practice and repetition as primary ways to teach and reinforce spelling.

A typical elementary school teacher uses a Monday through Friday spelling schedule with a new spelling list introduced on Monday and the spelling test administered on Friday. As a parent, you might have experienced this type of spelling homework schedule from your child's teacher:

- ♦ Monday: write your words ten times each.
- ♦ Tuesday: write each word in a sentence.
- ♦ Wednesday: alphabetize your list and write each word five times using a different colored pencil.
- ♦ Thursday: complete a crossword puzzle or word search using spelling words.
- ♦ Friday: take the spelling test.

DOI: 10.4324/9781003473879-4

While this approach works well for many students, it often does not fully help children with dysgraphia. The traditional methods for teaching spelling lack the direct and explicit instruction that is needed to help students with dysgraphia and written expression learning disabilities.

Our English language is an irregular language which complicates spelling and reading. Just try to sound out the word "was" or "color." These are two words that are not phonetically pronounceable. The English language has 26 letters that make up 44 sounds. Thus, spelling instruction is more complicated than teaching your child one-to-one letter-sound correspondences. The English writing system has three layers that affect spelling:

- ◆ Alphabetic layer: children learn letter-to-sound relationships.
- ◆ Pattern layer: children learn to find patterns that identify groups of letters (sometimes called word families).
- ◆ Meaning layer: children learn groups of letters to give word meanings.

As your child progresses through these layers, spelling difficulty increases since your child moves from spelling sounds to spelling for meaning.

Many children with dysgraphia also have accompanying learning disabilities such as dyslexia, which interferes with spelling. Other children have a weak memory system so they might learn the words through repetition and practice and pass their weekly spelling test only to forget how to spell the words a short time later. Thus, your child's spelling test grade might not accurately reflect their spelling accuracy in everyday writing. We want to help you help your child employ learning strategies, explicit and multisensory instruction, and fun activities to reinforce becoming a better speller. However, before we get ahead of ourselves, let's identify what the research reports on effective spelling instruction.

What the Research Reports

Perhaps you have considered the question, "Does spelling still matter and should schools continue teaching it?" It's a question that makes sense given today's technological society. Critics of spelling instruction often argue the points that incorrect spelling is not penalized on many standardized tests, technologies such as spell check and autocorrect reduce the importance of good spelling, and the various ways to spell words in casual forms of communication decrease the importance of correct spelling.

Researchers Pan et al. (2021) posed and answered the question, "Does spelling still matter and if so, how should it be taught?" by stating, "Overall, an abundance of research confirms that spelling remains important in the 21st century" (p. 1529). They indicated that spelling matters from the employment sector to the perceptions of writers, and even in online settings. For example, spelling errors on a job application can result in immediate rejection of one's application. They also revealed the most effective way to teach spelling is through direct and explicit teaching.

There are positive effects of formally teaching spelling. Graham and Santangelo (2014) completed a meta-analysis of 53 studies of students in kindergarten through twelfth grade and reported spelling gains were maintained over time and generalized to students' writing. They also reported students in these studies also made improvements in phonological awareness and reading skills.

There are two primary approaches to teaching spelling: explicit instruction and incidental instruction. For students with learning disabilities or spelling struggles, explicit instruction is the better of the two approaches (Williams et al., 2017; Graham, 2008; Pan et al., 2021). Explicit spelling instruction includes teaching phonological awareness, phonics for spelling, spelling rules, strategies for spelling unknown words, reteaching skills and strategies, word sorting, and reinforcement strategies.

Learning strategy instruction also helps children learn their spelling words. Joseph and colleagues (2012) completed a meta-analytic review of 31 studies that used the Cover-Copy-Compare

(CCC) strategy or its variations. The findings supported this procedure, as it was effective in helping students learn spelling as well as math facts. The authors reported that students received even more benefits when the CCC strategy was paired with token economies, goal setting, and opportunities to respond. They wrote, "When students practiced spelling words multiple times, they were able to meet mastery criteria in fewer sessions than when they spelled words only one at a time" (p. 124).

Graham (1983) reported on seven evidence-based practices for teaching spelling in schools. These included the test-study-test method whereby teachers give a pretest, students study words they missed, and students are retested and any missed words are incorporated into future lessons. Second, under adult supervision, students correct their misspellings by writing the correct spelling. Third, teach students a proven word study method for studying spelling words rather than allowing students to devise their own methods. Fourth, present spelling words in a list or column rather than in a sentence or paragraph. Fifth, present words in a whole rather than in a syllable format. Six, spelling games promote student interest. Seven, spend 60–75 minutes per week on spelling.

In terms of the spelling of students with learning disabilities, Williams and colleagues (2107) completed a meta-analysis of ten studies. These studies used self-correction procedures such as Cover-Copy-Compare or explicit instruction. All studies showed that students demonstrated increased spelling accuracy, although some not to clinically significant levels.

You might suggest to your child's special education teacher that they use a formal and explicit spelling program such as the Spelling Mastery Program. Darch and colleagues (2006) reported students using this program performed better than students without explicit instruction. The Spelling Mastery Program was also effective when a paraprofessional was trained on how to use the program to teach spelling (Owens et al., 2004). Spelling Mastery provides scripted lessons and explicit spelling instruction for students in first through sixth grades.

Quick Start Guide to Using Spelling

Teach a strategy. Empower your child by teaching a strategy they can use to practice learning spelling and vocabulary words. The Cover-Copy-Compare (CCC) strategy is appropriate for students in grades two and above. The steps include:

- ◆ C: Correct. The correct spelling of a word is viewed and studied.
- ◆ C: Cover. Cover the word, and write it from memory.
- ◆ C: Compare. Uncover the word, and check to see if your spelling matches the correct spelling.

If the word is spelled correctly, your child goes on to the next word using the same steps. If your child spelled the word incorrectly, have your child rewrite the word following the same CCC procedures.

A variation of the CCC strategy with one additional step is the Model-Cover-Copy- -Compare (MCCC) strategy:

- ◆ M: look at and *copy* the word (the correct "model" spelling is studied).
- ◆ C: look at and *study* the correct spelling.
- ◆ C: cover the word and *write* it from memory.
- ◆ C: *check* to see if the word was written correctly.

Follow the same process as written above if the word is spelled correctly or incorrectly.

Another learning strategy to teach your child is the SPELLER strategy. The steps for SPELLER include:

S: Spot the word and say it aloud.
P: Picture the word with your eyes open.
E: Eyes closed, visualize the word.
L: Open your eyes, and look to see if you are right.
L: Look away and write the word.
E: Examine it and check for correct spelling
R: Repeat or rewind.

Use multisensory approaches and games. Your child can learn spelling words while moving, talking, seeing, listening, using color, and playing games.

◆ Consider using the game Twister. Place the mat on the floor. Each time your child spins the spinner they spell a spelling word aloud as they move from dot to dot.

◆ Play hopscotch spelling. Draw a hopscotch board on the floor. Number your child's spelling list. Your child rolls a dice or spins a spinner. They identify their spelling word associated with the number rolled and hop into and over the squares as they spell the word aloud.

◆ Play spelling catch. Use a soft object that can be tossed back and forth between you and your child. Choose a spelling word, and then you and your child spell it aloud. Take turns with each person saying a letter aloud and then toss the ball.

◆ Use bouncing ball spelling. You say a spelling word for your child to spell. Your child uses a ball that bounces and says a letter each time they bounce and catch the ball.

◆ Play "pop it" spelling. Look online and purchase the alphabet Pop It fidget toy. Tell your child a spelling word. They spell it aloud while pressing the correct Pop It letter.

◆ Use Play-Doh. Purchase various colors of Play-Doh and roll and shape it into letters to spell words.

◆ Sand-board spelling. Use a cookie sheet with an edge. Purchase kinetic sand and place it on the tray. Tell your child a word to spell and they can use a finger to spell it in the sand.

◆ Try mesh spelling. Look online for cross-stitch sheets or plastic mesh sheets. Place the mesh sheet on a table. Place your child's writing paper on top of the mesh sheet. Tell your child a word to spell and they use a crayon or writing utensil to write as they say each letter aloud. The mesh sheet provides a "bumpy" tactile experience.

◆ Shaving cream spelling. This approach can be slightly messy, but you can reduce the mess by using a gallon bag that will seal. Place shaving cream in bag, on a tray, or tile wall against the bathtub. State a spelling word, and your child spells it in the shaving cream.

Obtain the list early accommodation. Children with dysgraphia often benefit from extra time to learn their spelling words, so if your child has an accommodation plan or IEP, request it be documented that your child receives his or her spelling words on the Friday preceding the weekend. This gives you and your child extra days to practice learning the words.

Ask for a reduced spelling list accommodation. If your child has difficulty memorizing, you can request your child receive the accommodation of reduced spelling words. For example, if the class has 20 spelling words, your child would be responsible for learning the first ten words. Then, for the spelling test, your child takes the test on all 20 words because you don't want your child to be embarrassed for only writing ten words and then sitting idly while the remainder of the class finishes the test. The teacher grades your child only on the words they studied or numbers 1–10.

Summary

Spelling remains an important academic skill for children to learn. Direct and explicit spelling instruction is most effective for children with dysgraphia. This type of approach includes teaching phonological awareness, phonics for spelling, spelling rules, strategies for spelling unknown words, reteaching skills and strategies, word sorting, and reinforcement strategies. The Cover-Copy-Compare learning strategy is an effective way to help children learn to spell. Teachers might use the Spelling Mastery Program whereas parents can use learning strategies or games to help promote their child's interest and engagement in spelling.

Resources

https://www.mheducation.com/prek-12/program/spelling-mastery/ MKTSP-UTC03M0.html: Spelling Mastery Spelling Program

https://www.spellingcity.com: Spelling City
https://www.kineticsand.com: Kinetic Sand
www.Amazon.com: Pop it Alphabet Version & Mesh Sheets

References

Darch, C., Eaves, R. C., Crowe, D. A., Simmons, K., & Conniff, A. (2006). Teaching spelling to students with learning disabilities: A comparison of rule-based strategies versus traditional instruction. *Journal of Direct Instruction, 6*(1), 1–16.

Graham, S. (1983). Effective spelling instruction. *The Elementary School Journal, 83*(5), 560–567.

Graham, S., Morphy, P., Harris, K. R., Fink-Chorzempa, B., Saddler, B., Moran, S., & Mason, L. (2008). Teaching spelling in the primary grades: A national survey of instructional practices and adaptations. *American Educational Research Journal, 45*(3), 796–825.

Graham, S., & Santangelo, T. (2014). Does spelling instruction make students better spellers, readers, and writers? A meta-analytic review. *Reading and Writing, 27*, 1703–1743.

Joseph, L. M., Konrad, M., Cates, G., Vajcner, T., Eveleigh, E., & Fishley, K. M. (2012). A meta-analytic review of the cover-copy-compare and variations of this self-management procedure. *Psychology in the Schools, 49*(2), 122–136.

Owens, S. H., Fredrick, L. D., & Shippen, M. E. (2004). Training a paraprofessional to implement "spelling mastery" and examining its effectiveness for students with learning disabilities. *Journal of Direct Instruction, 4*(2), 153–172.

Pan, S. C., Rickard, T. C., & Bjork, R. A. (2021). Does spelling still matter—And if so, how should it be taught? Perspectives from contemporary and historical research. *Educational Psychology Review, 33*, 1–30.

Williams, K. J., Walker, M. A., Vaughn, S., & Wanzek, J. (2017). A synthesis of reading and spelling interventions and their effects on spelling outcomes for students with learning disabilities. *Journal of Learning Disabilities, 50*(3), 286–297.

5

Strategies for Improving Penmanship and Handwriting

Penmanship Explained

The Cambridge Dictionary defines penmanship as "the ability to write neatly; or the activity of learning to do this" (2023). Although simply defined, penmanship is actually quite complex. The physical act of writing requires a number of mental and physical processes to be activated all at once. Specifically, *the ability to write neatly* requires one to have (Keller, 2001):

◆ Visual, auditory, and visuomotor perception skills.
◆ Gross/fine motor skills.
◆ Directionality skills.
◆ Sequencing skills.
◆ Recall skills
◆ Letter knowledge.
◆ Hand strength.
◆ Correct posture/paper position.
◆ Tracing/copying skills.
◆ Joining letters/cursive script.
◆ Self-evaluation skills.

Further, the *activity of learning to write* requires a simultaneous focus on four different aspects of writing

DOI: 10.4324/9781003473879-5

◆ Pencil grasp (positioning of fingers on writing utensil).
◆ Letter formation (script and cursive).
◆ Legibility (spacing).
◆ Pacing (fluency and pressure).

Given the interconnectedness of these broad skill sets and the complexity of the processes needed to write legibly, it is not surprising that penmanship is both difficult to learn and difficult to teach! Contributing to the problem, there has been a decreased emphasis on penmanship in mainstream educational settings in recent years (Shaturaev, 2019). So, it is possible your child has not benefited from systematic or consistent handwriting instruction prior to this diagnosis. It is also true that children today tend to gravitate more toward iPhones and iPads than pencils and crayons at earlier ages in our increasingly technology-rich households. Consequently, there are often fewer opportunities to practice the formative handwriting skills listed above during everyday play activities than was typical in a pre-smart device society. As these skills build upon one another over time, these generational changes may make it harder for our children to *write neatly*, than it was for us.

No judgment! Smart devices have unique benefits and provide wonderful learning and enrichment opportunities for young children (Harwood, 2017). We point this out only to encourage you to bring the pencils, paper, and crayons back to the table and to dispel any doubts you may have about the importance of handwriting practice for children with and without dysgraphia.

Don't Write Off Handwriting!

It is true that in today's society, most written communication occurs through typing on laptops or texting on smartphones. As adults, it is not uncommon to go days at a time without having to put a real-life pen to paper. So, this begs the question… how important is good penmanship anyway? The truth is that writing by hand the old-fashioned way is still an essential and unavoidable life skill. Take a moment to consider how many ways you use the handwritten word to organize your life:

- ◆ Posting reminders.
- ◆ Jotting down lists.
- ◆ Note-taking.
- ◆ Thank you notes.
- ◆ Journaling.
- ◆ Labeling.

How many times have you heard people making fun of doctors' rushed handwriting and impossible-to-read prescriptions... giving the impression that their care is rushed and not prioritized? If your child's teacher sent home a handwritten message you could not easily read, how much confidence would you have in his or her teaching ability? Messy handwriting distracts from the message and can lead to pre-judgments about the messenger.

In employment settings, illegible writing can reflect poorly on performance if perceived as unprofessional, disorganized, or indicative of a lack of care or commitment to a given task. In general, messy handwriting makes it difficult for readers to trust the knowledge and intended communication of the unskilled writer. For these reasons, and many others, handwriting should not be dismissed as merely a "lost art" in the age of instantaneous handheld technology.

Isn't There an App for That?

Probably... yes! However, access to reliable technology is never a given, and in our fast-paced adult lives, we cannot take for granted the ability to communicate through the handwritten word when we need to. Although our handwriting may lack formality in everyday use, there is a general conformity to the rules of penmanship we were taught in childhood that has allowed us to become fluent communicators in writing.

So, even in the age of high-tech devices, spell check, and artificial intelligence... good-enough penmanship is still required to effectively express and organize oneself in both personal and professional settings. Therefore, opportunities to "put the pencil to the paper" should be enhanced for children with dysgraphia, even when more high-tech writing methods are more accessible and, likely, more preferred.

Penmanship Matters, and Here is Why!

Put simply, labored writing is a major "brain drain." When children struggle to maintain a good pencil grasp, position the paper properly, or form joining letters legibly, they fatigue quickly and frustrate easily. Further, the most up-to-date professional research tells us that poor handwriting can lead to poor academic achievement overall (Grajo et al., 2020).

It is true that technology can and should help children with one or more aspects of writing described here so they can maintain endurance where it counts most. However, in addition to introducing compensatory strategies to prevent writing fatigue, we also want to emphasize the benefits of improving penmanship to whatever extent possible. This perspective is based on the understanding that "the physical act of writing" is correlated with improved memory and focus, as well as improved performance in core academic areas such as spelling, reading, and math (Grajo et al., 2020). As children's ability to handwrite letters has been linked to their ability to process visual letters, handwriting is particularly impactful on early literacy skills (McCloskey & Rapp, 2017). Here, we provide you with a brief summary of the research describing the relationship between common recommendations for handwriting instruction for children with and without dysgraphia to help you know what to look for in a quality program.

What the Research Reports

ALL Students Need More Handwriting Instruction

The preponderance of research focused on handwriting instruction confirms two indisputable facts (Graham et al., 2001; Grajo et al., 2020; Santangelo & Graham, 2016):

1. Handwriting must be explicitly taught.
2. Handwriting must be frequently practiced.

A 2016 comprehensive meta-analysis of handwriting instruction for students in K-12 settings conducted by Santangelo and

Graham confirmed this, finding statistically significant differences in the writing skills of study participants who received explicit instruction compared to those who did not. The researchers reported improved legibility, quality, length, and fluency when a) individualized instruction and b) technology-enhanced instruction were provided to students. These findings are consistent with a larger body of research indicating a need to reprioritize handwriting instruction for all students, to prevent the pervasive handwriting deficits that contribute to diminished educational outcomes for so many.

A Framework for Supporting Students with Specific Learning Disabilities

To support educators in their efforts to prevent and remediate the writing deficits of children identified with specific learning disabilities, Graham and colleagues recommended six guiding principles (Graham et al., 2001):

1. Provide quality writing instruction.
2. Tailor instruction to meet the individual's need.
3. Intervene early.
4. Expect that every child can learn to write.
5. Identify and address roadblocks to writing.
6. Employ technology.

Occupational Therapy: What Works?

In the case of children with dysgraphia who are found eligible for special education services, handwriting instruction will most often be supported by an occupational therapist (OT). Or, you may decide to access OT services for your child privately to increase the intensity and frequency of exposure to quality instruction given the consensus in the professional literature discussed here. In an effort to establish best practices for OTs, Grajo and colleagues (2020) conducted a systematic review of the professional literature to determine what methods OTs were using to increase children's academic participation.

Here, the authors reported findings specific to handwriting instruction that support the continued use of therapeutic practices that involve traditional paper-pencil activities coupled with cognitive-behavioral interventions including self-evaluation techniques and specific performance feedback. The authors also emphasized the need to connect prerequisite skill training directly to writing tasks, rather than isolating component skills and addressing them outside the writing context using sensori-motor techniques alone (Grajo et al., 2020).

Handwriting Without Tears

As briefly discussed in Chapter 3, Handwriting without Tears (by Learning without Tears) is a commonly used and research-supported program developed by occupational therapist Jan Z. Olsen. This program is typically delivered by trained OTs in school and clinical settings. A link to the large body of evidence supporting the use of this comprehensive commercial program with children with writing challenges is provided in the resource section of this chapter. Here, we would like to highlight the core features of the program that, combined, have consistently produced the desired results. These include:

- ◆ A developmental approach.
- ◆ A multisensory, physical approach.
- ◆ A focus on cursive connection, joining letters.
- ◆ Provision of teacher support, professional development for program implementation.

Quick Start Guide to Supporting Your Child's Penmanship

It is clear in the research that systematic and explicit handwriting instruction is required to improve penmanship. Knowing this, you can better advocate for your child in educational settings to ensure your child has focused goals and direct instruction related to the four aspects of handwriting discussed here (grasp, formation, legibility, pacing). You can also share the checklist of best practices for handwriting instruction created by researchers Graham and Harris provided in the resource section at the end of this chapter. This is an excellent resource prompting educators to self-evaluate the extent to which they incorporate best practices in their daily instruction. This is also a great reference for parents to know what to look for in a quality writing program for their child with dysgraphia. Knowing what specific deficits your child is presenting with at any given time and the best practices for focused intervention will help you make informed decisions on how to help your child make progress.

While the trained specialists are working with your child in a more formalized way in the school and/or clinical settings, you can support handwriting development in the home with less formality by providing supplemental activities better suited for parent's facilitation. The goal should be to:

- Increase opportunities to practice penmanship.
- Provide varying ways to engage in handwriting practice.
- Promote engagement, enjoyment, and self-confidence.
- Informally monitor progress toward handwriting proficiency over time.
- Minimize frustration.

To help you achieve these goals, we recommend the following strategies for improving penmanship in the home through naturally occurring and enjoyable daily activities:

Practice With a Purpose

- Write a list of preferred snacks for the week.
- Copy a list of ingredients needed to bake cookies together.
- Make a list of places you want to visit together.
- Make holiday cards.
- Write thank you cards.
- Leave family members notes.
- Write pen pal letters to a family or friend.
- Write steps to complete a chore.
- Start daily journaling together.

Take a Multisensory Approach

♦ Play tic-tac-toe using letters.
♦ Complete connect-the-dots.
♦ Create simple crossword puzzles based on your child's interests.
♦ Complete Mad-libs together.
♦ Practice letter writing in shaving cream, rice, flour, or sand.
♦ Practice letter formation with play-dough, pipe cleaners, etc.
♦ Trace letters on sandpaper or other tactile materials.
♦ Use rainbow writing (copy letters/words overlapping colored ink).
♦ Use fun stamps between words to practice spacing.
♦ Trace Scrabble tiles.
♦ Do mazes.
♦ Use color-changing markers.
♦ Use finger paint.
♦ Use sidewalk chalk.
♦ Use letter formation rhymes.

Build a Writing Tool Kit

♦ Pencil grips.
♦ Specialty writing utensils.
♦ Slant board.
♦ Clipboard.
♦ Lined paper.
♦ Highlighters.
♦ Graph paper.
♦ Posters showing letters and print and cursive.
♦ Motivating characters or favorite color writing utensils.

Leverage Technology

Sound counterintuitive? It is not, as long as high-tech supports are used to supplement not supplant daily handwriting practice. There are a number of highly interactive apps, games, and programs designed for handwriting support that you may want to review and test out to determine the appropriateness and usefulness for your child. Although the goal is to increase your child's opportunities to write by hand, technology can be very motivating for children and keep them engaged in writing-related activities for longer periods of time. Throughout this book, we highlight programs and apps that you may want to consider to enhance writing overall. Here, we provide you with just a few examples of apps designed to motivate children to practice handwriting through fun and engaging activities. As technological preferences differ between households and these types of resources are continuously being updated and improved, be sure to do your research to find the most up-to-date, age-appropriate, and highly rated options available now.

App/Program	Website Description
Cursive Writing Wizard by L'Escapadou	A tool to help children learn how to trace their letters and numbers, designed to maintain motivation.
Crazy Cursive Letters by MadeByEducators	Provides children with practice in writing the top 100 words in cursive. Children can and can also enter their own words to practice.
Touch and Write by FIZZBRAIN LLC	Recreates the fun multisensory strategies commonly used in classrooms such as learning letter formation by writing with shaving cream, Jell-O, finger paint, etc.
iTrace by Michael Bogorad	Adjusts the difficulty of letter tracing to provide an appropriate level of challenge as children's ability progresses. After each exercise, children are rewarded with a short game. The activity change is designed to keep them engaged.
Spooky Letters by MadeByEducators	Allows children to practice letter forming in both cursive and pre-cursive format. Letters are also sounded out phonetically.

Summary

Here, we provide you the rationale for focusing on penmanship to improve your child's overall academic achievement in addition to introducing the most appropriate technological supports they may need to become proficient writers. Knowing the consensus across years of research supporting both explicit and multisensory approaches can help discriminate between what does and does not work to develop children's penmanship skills and encourage you to advocate for methods that will produce results and keep your child motivated and engaged.

Resources

HWTEfficacy_1.17.19_web.pdf (lwtears.com) Handwriting Without Tears Research Review

Kids love these 10 Games for Handwriting Practice (wootherapy.com) Games for Handwriting Practice

Want to Improve Children's Writing? Don't Neglect Their Handwriting by Steve Graham, American Educator Winter 2009–10, American Federation of Teachers (aft.org) Checklist for Best Practices in Handwriting Instruction

7 Reasons Why Handwriting Is Important for Kids | Highlights for Children 7 Reasons Why Handwriting is Important for Kids

References

Graham, S., Harris, K. R., & Larsen, L. (2001). Prevention and intervention of writing difficulties for students with learning disabilities. *Learning Disabilities Research & Practice, 16*(2), 74–84.

Grajo, L. C., Candler, C., & Sarafian, A. (2020). Interventions within the scope of occupational therapy to improve children's academic participation: A systematic review. *The American Journal of Occupational Therapy, 74*(2). 7402180030p1–7402180030p32.

Harwood, D. (2017). Crayons and iPads: Learning and teaching of young children in the digital world. *Crayons and iPads*, 1–152.

Keller, M. (2001). Handwriting club: Using sensory integration strategies to improve handwriting. *Intervention in School and Clinic, 37*(1), 9–12.

Santangelo, T., Graham, S. (2016). A comprehensive meta-analysis of handwriting instruction. *Educ Psychol Rev, 28*, 225–265. https://doi.org/10.1007/s10648-015-9335-1

Shaturaev, J. (2019). The importance of handwriting in education. *International Journal of Advanced Research, 7*(12), 947–954.

6

Strategies for Writing

The Writing Process Explained

There are many parts to what makes up "writing." When you think about what goes into writing a paper or a story, it is a complex cognitive process. First, children need to be able to use fine motor skills to take a pencil to paper or to use a keyboard to create sentences. Children also need the language to identify and order words in sentences and sentences in paragraphs as well as the ability to decide the order of events in a story.

In addition, your child's memory is a crucial component in the ability to be able to write well (Harris & Graham, 2013). Memory is organized into three areas:

- ◆ Short-term memory.
- ◆ Long-term memory.
- ◆ Working memory.

Short-term memory refers to the part of your memory you use when you are doing a quick task such as copying from the board. Long-term memory is used to remember information that is stored for long-term retrieval such as remembering previous events or experiences to write a story (Spencer, 2015). Last, working memory is a key part of the writing process. When students need to stop to remember how to spell a word or form a letter,

DOI: 10.4324/9781003473879-6

this puts an immense strain on a child's cognitive load. Cognitive load refers to the burden that is placed upon working memory when they are completing tasks that are not necessarily automatic (Willingham, 2017).

As your child is learning how to write, the first things you may notice are the "skills," which include handwriting, using proper punctuation, spacing between words, and remembering to capitalize the beginning of proper nouns and the first words in sentences. The next part of what makes up "writing" is knowledge about how and what to write. This includes understanding how to write a letter vs. how to write a story. Different *strategies* are used based on what the purpose is for writing. Strategies are the "how" of writing including teaching students how to organize, revise, and edit their writing. Last, is keeping your child motivated to write. Part of keeping your child motivated is helping them track their own progress as well as making writing meaningful for your child by offering a variety of authentic writing tasks.

You can help support your child at home by understanding how the writing process is taught in school. The most common way that teachers teach students how to write is some form of the writing process. There is not one definition of the writing process, but most often it is made up of some version of the following. The writing process consists of children planning what they will write, drafting their writing pieces, revising the content, editing for spelling or grammar, and finally publishing (Calkins, 1983; Graves, 1983). It is also important to remember that the writing process is not necessarily linear. For example, your child could be asked to write about their favorite food. Perhaps they start planning and choose "pizza." But while planning for pizza, another idea came to their mind, such as ice cream. Maybe they start over and begin the planning phase again. Many times children go from one step to the next or maybe even skip a step, based on how they think they are doing on the task. You can certainly see why the process is complex!

TABLE 6.1 The Writing Process

Step	Description
Planning	Students think of an idea for the purpose of their writing. They plan what they want to write. Oftentimes they use a graphic organizer or outline.
Drafting	Students begin to take what they planned and start composing sentences and paragraphs.
Editing	Once students have a draft, they edit their writing. They check for punctuation and spelling.
Revising	Students may read their paper and decide that they want to revise or change organizational components. Perhaps they move a sentence from here to there.
Publishing	Students rewrite their drafts into a final copy.

What the Research Reports

For most students, the writing process is "powerful" enough for them to become competent writers (Graham & Sandmel, 2011). However, children with dysgraphia will often need some type of explicit instruction *as well as* instruction in the writing process. Students with dysgraphia, or learning disabilities, often struggle with many parts of the writing process. These include the ability to come up with ideas, put those ideas into organized sentences on paper or type them onto the computer, and revise, edit, and publish (Graham & Harris, 2003; Troia, 2006; Hashey et al., 2020).

What to look for? How would you know, specifically, what areas your child may need support in? First of all, if they have difficulty with handwriting and spelling, this often indicates they may be struggling in the area of writing instruction. This includes that their handwriting or typing may be slower than their peers. Students also may have difficulty with motivation for writing. If a task is hard, it certainly is more difficult to stay motivated. This can directly affect their confidence. In addition, students may lack knowledge of the writing process as well as the different genres of writing. They may not be able to know how to complete the writing task, and they may get "stuck" and frustrated because they are not sure what to do next (Graham & Perin, 2007).

So, what does the research say about what works for teaching writing to students with learning disabilities? Research shows that the following had an impact on the writing of students with learning disabilities which include: strategy instruction, dictation, use of procedural facilitators, or graphic organizers, goal setting, and process writing (Gillespie & Graham, 2014). Let's talk about each of these recommendations with *what* they are as well as some examples.

Process Writing

The writing process, which was mentioned above, has been found to be effective for students with dysgraphia as well as positive effects for all students. Most teachers use some form of the writing process. You may also hear the term "writer's workshop." When teachers use this approach for teaching, many students are successful. This approach has been found to be successful for some students with learning disabilities, but many in fact require some other type of intervention in addition to the writing process approach.

Procedural Facilitation and Prewriting Strategies

Procedural facilitators (PFs) are graphic organizers that are designed to break down the writing task into smaller steps. PFs have been found to be effective in increasing writing quality for both students with and without disabilities (Flanagan et al., 2016; Launder et al., 2022). The example below shows the use of PF for opinion writing. You can see that there are visuals to help children see where and what to write about in each part of the PF. Prewriting involves activities for organizing and planning written drafts. Graphic organizers include word webs, outlining, or answering prompts prior to writing. The use of some type of prewriting strategy has been shown to be effective for students with learning disabilities.

TABLE 6.2 Example of Procedural Facilitator

Write a paragraph. Share your opinion:

What is your opinion about the topic? (just a few words).

| |
| |

	Topic Sentence: A complete sentence that tells about your opinion on the topic.
	Give 2 reasons for your opinion (just a few words):

Conclusion

Conclusion sentence: This is a complete sentence that wraps up everything in your paragraph.

| |
| |

Used with permission (Launder, S. 2022)

Explicit Strategy Instruction

Strategies are tools or "tricks" to help support children in completing parts of the writing process. Explicit and systematic strategy instruction has been shown to increase the writing ability of both students with and without disabilities in elementary and secondary settings (Graham et al., 2012; Graham & Perin, 2007; Miller & Spencer, 2017). What is explicit and systematic instruction? This refers to the instruction that is clear, meaning students directly understand what they are learning, and the learning is taught in a structured, systematic way in which skills are built upon each other and mastered.

Children can be taught strategies to help them across various parts of the writing process such as prewriting, drafting, revising, and editing their work. For example, children with dysgraphia often struggle with organizing their thoughts and getting them onto paper clearly. By using a strategy to support their organization and planning, they are able to then draft better-written pieces. It breaks the task down into smaller, more manageable parts. Using checklists, graphic organizers, and teaching students how to use what strategy are all parts of effective strategic instruction.

Self-Regulated Strategy Development (SRSD) is an evidence-based practice for teaching strategies and has been found to be very effective in teaching writing to students with learning disabilities (Graham & Harris, 2013). SRSD is a framework that teachers use to help students improve their writing. There are several "steps" when teaching students a learning strategy. Each step is taught across a series of lessons. One common strategy that students use in opinion writing is "POW + TREE." POW + TREE is described below:

P	Pick a Topic
O	Organize with TREE
W	Write and Organize my Notes
T	Topic Sentence
R	Reasons
E	Explain
E	Ending

The first is to **develop background knowledge**. This is where you help your child understand the purpose of writing as well as the parts of the mnemonic you are trying to teach them. Using the example above, you would want them to understand what an opinion is as well as a strategy. The second step is to **discuss the strategy**. You want to teach them the mnemonic name as well as *when and why* they would use it. Children also learn why this strategy would benefit them. The third step is to **model it**, where students watch the teacher or instructor explicitly model the steps of the strategy. This step is important and may have to be repeated. Throughout all of the steps, children **memorize it**, meaning they should know the steps as well as each component of the mnemonic. The next stage is **support it**, where children are ready to practice the strategy. They should be provided with many opportunities to practice the strategy. And last, **establish independent practice**, when students are able to use the strategy independently.

Another key part of SRSD instruction is **goal setting** and **self-statements**. These are two powerful components of this specific strategy, and **goal setting** has been shown in the research to increase the quality of student writing (Graham & Perin, 2007). When students set goals, they are more likely to achieve the goals they have set. Self-statements are made with the child to individualize what they should do when they get "stuck" across any part of the process. For example, instead of saying "I can't do this!" when they are stuck, teachers model for them to say something instead, such as "I know I can do this. I know the strategies. Let me take a deep breath and start again." These self-statements are individualized to help students based on their individual needs. For more information on SRSD instruction, there are resources listed at the end of this chapter.

Dictation

Dictation is the act of speaking to a scribe or an electronic tool to get written output. By using technology tools to support students with dysgraphia, students can focus on the *content*, rather than on the spelling of each individual word.

Quick Start for Using Writing Strategies to Support Dysgraphia

Now that you understand what has been found to be effective for children with dysgraphia within the research, you can advocate on his or her behalf to make sure they are receiving quality instruction and interventions to support their writing ability.

Here are some recommendations for how you can support your child at home.

Talk to the teacher. Use the same language: your child's teacher is likely using the writing process approach, or some variation of it. When you meet with your child's teacher, discuss *how* they teach writing in their classroom. Ask your child's teacher if there are any areas in which they struggle and find out some ways you can support this at home.

Set goals. Setting goals and monitoring your child's progress can be powerful. Perhaps they are struggling with the *time* in which they spend writing. Help build stamina by having them write for a set amount of time. It doesn't necessarily have to be paper/pencil writing. Let them word process or use dictation tools. Monitor how long they spent on the writing task. Mark this down on a piece of paper or make a graph. As they continue to practice writing as well as learning their strategies, count and record the number of words. Praise them for progress and set goals for incentives. You can also try monitoring the number of words they wrote and watch them progress in that area.

Practice using technology. Have your child try out some dictation tools, such as speech-to-text on their computer or the voice-to-text function on their phones, they are more apt to focus on the meaning or message than on the spelling and grammar components of their writing. Make sure to have them use a graphic organizer before they begin "speaking" into the device. It is important to reinforce that they still have to plan before they use their dictation tools to ensure they are organizing their writing.

Summary

By understanding what and how your child is taught how to write, you can better support them at home. It is also important to ask questions to make sure that your child is receiving quality writing interventions in the area of writing at school. Keep a clear line of communication open with your child's teacher. Use some of the resources and strategies that are supported by research to support your child's writing at home.

Resources

www.thinkSRSD.com Professional Development Courses to Learn the SRSD in Writing Strategies

www.srsdonline.org Online Teacher Training in the Areas of SRSD. There Are Also Links to Free Resources.

https://www.readingrockets.org/reading-101/reading-and-writing-basics/writing Reading Rockets: Basics of the Writing Process Module

References

Calkins, L. M. (1983). *Lesson from a child: On the teaching and learning of writing*. Heinemann.

Flanagan, S., Bouck, E. C., & Cutter, E. (2016). Wright right: Improving and sustaining written expression abilities in middle school students with and without learning disabilities using procedural facilitators. *Learning Disabilities: A Multidisciplinary Journal, 21*(1), 68–79. https://doi.org/10.18666/LDMJ-2016-V21-I1-6742

Gillespie, A., & Graham, S. (2014). A meta-analysis of writing interventions for students with learning disabilities, *Exceptional Children, 80*(4), 454–473. https://doi.org/10.1177/0014402914527238

Graham, S., & Harris, K. (2003). Students with learning disabilities and the process of writing: A meta-analysis of SRSD studies. In H.L. Swanson, K. R. Harris, & S. Graham (Eds.) *Handbook of learning disabilities* (pp. 323–344). Guilford Press.

Graham, S., McKeown, D., Kiuhara, S., & Harris, K. R. (2012). A meta-analysis of writing instruction for students in the elementary grades. *Journal of Educational Psychology, 104*(4), 879–896.

Graham, S., & Perin. D. (2007a). A meta-analysis of writing instruction for adolescent students. *Journal of Educational Psychology, 99*(3), 445–476.

Graham, S., & Sandmel, K. (2011). The process writing approach: A meta-analysis. *The Journal of Educational Research, 104*(6), 396–407. https://doi.org/10.1080/00220671.2010.488703

Graves, D. (1983). *Writing: Teachers and children at work*. Heinemann.

Harris, K., & Graham, S. (2013). "An adjective is a word hanging down from a noun": Learning to write and students with learning disabilities. *Annals of Dyslexia, 63*(1), 65–79. https://doi.org/10.1007/s11881-011-0057-x

Hashey, A., Miller, K. M., & Foxworth, L. (2020). Combining universal design for learning and self-regulated strategy development to bolster writing instruction. *Intervention in School and Clinic, 56*(1), 22–28. https://doi.org/10.1177/1053451220910733

Launder, S. M., Miller, K. M., & Wood, J. (2022). Examining the impact of virtual procedural facilitator training on opinion writing of elementary school-age students with autism spectrum disorders. *Education & Training in Autism & Developmental Disabilities, 57*(2), 216–228.

Miller, K.M., & Spencer, S.A. (2017). When writing isn't easy or fun. In W. Murawski & K. James (Eds.), *What really works for special learners* (pp. 49–59). Corwin Press.

Spencer, S.A. (2015). *Making the common core writing standards accessible through universal design for learning.* Corwin Press.

Troia, G. (2006). Writing instruction for students with disabilities. In C. MacArthur, S. Graham, & J. Fitzgerald (Eds.), *Handbook of writing research* (pp. 324–336). Guilford Press.

Willingham, D. (2017). A mental model of the learner: Teaching the basic science of educational psychology to future teachers. *Mind, Brain and Education, 11*(4), 166–175.

7

Strategies for Making Writing Fun

Making Writing Fun Explained

Motivation for writing is key for students to be successful. As discussed in the previous chapter, the process of writing places major demands on both long-term and working memory (McCutchen, 1986; Philippakos et al., 2023). Motivation to write can substantially affect a student's writing performance as well as the degree to which students will continue to try or work on a writing task (Bruning & Horn, 2000; Graham et al., 2017b; Philippakos et al., 2023).

But how do we motivate students with dysgraphia to complete something that is very difficult for them? Just like it can be difficult to motivate adults to go to the gym after the holidays, so is the case to get dysgraphic students excited about writing. But the more we "work out," the easier it gets for adults. The same goes for writing; the more we do it, the "stronger" or better we become at it. So how do we get there? This chapter describes some activities you can do with your child to help motivate them, keep it fun, and keep them engaged while building their writing skills.

What the Research Reports

Students with learning disabilities, including those with dysgraphia, are engaged less and show less interest in writing than

DOI: 10.4324/9781003473879-7

their peers. They may not understand the purpose of writing and feel that their success is based on things out of their control. This can cause them to be disengaged in writing instruction (De La Paz et al., 2018). In addition, students with learning disabilities are more likely to have negative feelings such as anxiety or depression with the writing process (De La Paz, 2018; Santangelo, 2014). Self-efficacy, otherwise described as the confidence that children perceive when they have to perform a task, has been shown to be a strong predictor of achievement in middle school for students who are at risk or who have learning disabilities (Klassen, 2002). In fact, Graham and colleagues (2017b) found that students' attitudes toward writing and self-efficacy made an impact on their writing quality as well as on the length of their written drafts. There has also been research to support that there is a link between a student's attitude about writing and the positive impact on student writing performance. Researchers have also found that a writer's attitude, in children as young as third grade, can have an influence on their writing performance (DeSmedt et al., 2018).

It has been found that beliefs in our child's abilities can have an impact on our child's performance as well. For example, there is research on teacher expectations for students and their academic performance. Rubie-Davis and colleagues (2014) looked at students in preschool through grade four and compared the expectations the teachers had for their students and the impact on their academic achievement. This study did not specifically look at writing alone but looked at a variety of academic areas. If the teacher expected more from the student, the student achieved more than they otherwise would have, and if the teacher expected less, the student was more likely to achieve less (Julien, 2018; Rubie-Davis et al., 2014). Thus, it is critically important that we all have high expectations for our children but give them the support needed to be successful. So how will we do that? What are some ways we can make writing at home less strenuous and more fun? Some ideas below can help you begin to make writing fun for your dysgraphic child.

Quick Start Guide to Making Writing Fun

Make it authentic: Are you going grocery shopping? Getting your Amazon shopping list set for Christmas? Addressing cards for a party? These are all activities that require your child to write for real-life activities. Any activity that can practice the skills (e.g., handwriting, spelling, grammar) is great practice for writing fluency, or how fast they can physically write. Is your child upset that they don't allow phones during the school day? Are they upset that there is garbage on the beach? Practicing having them write letters to important people about the topic is a great way to get them to practice the opinion or argumentative writing genre. Do they like comic books? Have them practice writing and creating comic strips.

Make it social: There are so many great technology tools (more on that in the next chapter) that can be motivating and fun for your child. Have them create a social media blog (appropriate based on their age and audience) about whatever topic they wish. Give them opportunities to communicate with other family members or friends via writing. Let them text from their phone or device. The more social currency an activity has, the more likely your child will complete it.

It doesn't have to be TRADITIONAL: Remember those skills that make up the writing process? Organizing, drafting, publishing? Think about ways that your child can practice these skills at home. Many children with dysgraphia have difficulty with the traditional process of writing or the use of a pencil or keyboard. Instead of having them physically write, have them practice organizing or publishing their writing using other means. For example, with younger children, have them practice *planning* their narrative story via pictures about a topic, and they can *publish* their story by verbally telling it to you. Take it a step further and have them create a video on their device or phone. Get your child to type faster. Let them practice their typing by using a typing game for motivation.

Technology supports: Writing can be laborious and strenuous for the dysgraphic child. Use dictation tools to provide support. So instead of having them type or write part of the story, let them dictate it onto the computer or device or even to you!

Give them a choice: Let your child make a choice in what type of activity they would like to do, what topic they would write on, and who they would like to write to. Remember, if they get frustrated or are getting annoyed, it's always best to take a break and go back to the writing activity at another time.

Design a space: Create an area in your home that is their *writer's corner*. Let them pick the writing utensils, go for variety! Use pencils, crayons, markers, or whatever sparks their interest. Stock it with fun paper or notebooks. Help them feel ownership of this space which may motivate and spark their interest to write in that particular area.

Become a critic: Does your child like TV? Do they like to go to the movies? Are they into music? Have them write a review about whatever TV show they are watching, movie in the theater, or favorite new song. Model for them how to write a positive (or a negative) review.

Design something new: Is your child into recipes? Have them create or revise a new or traditional favorite food. Do they like games? Have them write instructions down for their friend or babysitter.

Keep it short: Writing is already a frustrating task for so many learners. By giving them opportunities to practice for just a few minutes a day, every day, you will build their persistence and skills without the added stress.

Share your writing: Model for your child how to write a letter, send a text, or make a list. Write a story together. You are your child's best model aside from the school day. There are letter-generating websites that can support the letter-writing process (see chart below).

Keep track of their progress: How many minutes have they worked on this from last week? More or less? Have them set goals and select incentives once they have met their goals. You may

TABLE 7.1 Technology Resources to Support Writing at Home Technology Resources to Support Writing at Home

Website	Description
StoryJumperhttps://www.storyjumper.com/	A website that allows your child to create and publish your child's book. There are options to order a print copy to read at home.
Read Write Think Letter Generator Toolhttps://www.readwritethink.org/classroom-resources/student-interactives/letter-generator	This tool allows students to generate a friendly or business letter by using prompts to guide students into letter writing.
Scholastic Story Startershttp://www.scholastic.com/teachers/story-starters/index.html	This tool provides ideas for writing prompts across different genres of writing.
Storybirdhttps://storybird.com/	An online tool that allows kids to create their own stories and pair them with artwork.
Typing Clubhttps://www.typingclub.com/	Use this online tool to have your child practice typing skills.
Rewards Charts: https://kidrewards.org/	A great way to monitor the amount of time your child has spent writing at home and to keep track of your child's goals.

want to set their goal to be easily attainable and increase it as they gain confidence.

Technology can be fun. Here are a few that can motivate and support your child at home. In the next chapter, there will be some technology apps and websites that can also support your child's writing progress at home.

Summary

Finding ways to motivate your child is critically important to get them to be interested in practicing writing skills at home. This chapter discussed specific research to support how a dysgraphic child's motivation directly impacts their writing performance. It is important to set high expectations for your child but give them support to be successful. This chapter offers practical tips to make writing fun and engaging for your dysgraphic child.

Resources

https://www.storyboardthat.com/comic-maker Comic Strip Maker
https://www.readingrockets.org/topics/writing/articles/7-great-ways
-encourage-your-childs-writing Reading Rockets

References

Bruning, R. H., & Horn, C. (2000). Developing motivation to write. *Educational Psychologist, 35*(1), 25–37. https://doi.org/10.1207/S15326985EP3501_4

De La Paz, S., & Butler, C. (2018). Promoting motivated writers: Suggestions for teaching and conducting research with students with learning disabilities and struggling learners. *Learning Disabilities: A Multidisciplinary Journal, 23*(2), 56–69. https://doi.org/10.18666/LDMJ-2018-V23-I2-9064

De Smedt, F., Merchie, E., Barendse, M., Rosseel, Y., De Naeghel, J., & Van Keer, H. (2018). Cognitive and motivational challenges in writing: Studying gender and achievement level. *Reading Research Quarterly, 53*(2), 249–272. https://doi.org/10.1002/rrq.193

Graham, S., Kiuhara, S. A., Harris, K. R., & Fishman, E. J. (2017b). The relationship among strategic writing behavior, writing motivation, and writing performance with young, developing writers. *The Elementary School Journal, 118*(1), 82–104. https://doi.org/10.1086/693009

Julien, K. (2018). Loving care and funky pens: Motivating young writers. *Reading Teacher, 71*(6), 659–668. https://doi.org/10.1002/trtr.1670

Klassen, R. (2002). Writing in early adolescence: A review of the role of self-efficacy beliefs. *Educational Psychology Review, 14,* 173–203.

McCutchen, D. (1986). Domain knowledge and linguistic knowledge in the development of writing ability. *Journal of Memory and Language, 25*(1), 431–444. https://doi.org/10.1016/0749- 596X(86)90036-7

Philippakos, W. C., & MacArthur, C. (2023). Writing motivation of college students in basic writing and first-year composition classes: Confirmatory factor analysis of scales on goals, self-efficacy, beliefs, and affect. *Journal of Learning Disabilities, 56*(1), 72–92. https://doi .org/10.1177/00222194211053238

Rubie-Davies, C. M., Weinstein, R. S., Huang, F. L., Gregory, A., Cowan, P. A., & Cowan, C. P. (2014). Successive teacher expectation effects across the early school years. *Journal of Applied Developmental Psychology, 35*(3), 181–191. https://doi. org/10.1016/j.appdev.2014.03.006

Santangelo, T. (2014). Why is writing so difficult for design of effective instruction? *LD: A Contemporary Journal, 12*(1), 5–20.

8

Technology for Dysgraphia

Assistive Technology Explained

Has your child been frustrated with the laborious task of putting pencil to paper? Have they crumpled their paper up? Has their handwriting been hard to read? You are not alone! Children with dysgraphia may have physical difficulties with the transcription process of writing. To help support these difficulties, you probably considered using technology. There continue to be ample types of technology in schools. It can be overwhelming, but with the right tools and information, you can feel empowered to bring forth information about your child to his or her IEP team for assistive technology (AT) consideration.

For students with dysgraphia, assistive technology is a critical way that support can be given to your child. AT can provide access to the curriculum content so that the areas in which your child struggles with writing do not interfere with the writing process. AT provides support, or an accommodation, so your child can learn the content and that their dysgraphia does not inhibit their ability to express themselves. So how do you get AT for your child?

Now, let's discuss the technology part. With so many technological choices, this can be overwhelming when considering the possibilities. Let's discuss the options and how they are

DOI: 10.4324/9781003473879-8

TABLE 8.1 Assistive Technology Defined

Term	Legislation	Definition	Example
Assistive Technology Device	Individuals with Disabilities Education Act (IDEA, 2004)	Any item, piece of equipment, or product system, whether acquired commercially off the shelf, modified, or customized that is used to increase, maintain, or improve the functional capabilities of a child with a disability. (IDEA, 2004, Section 300.5)	Speech-to-text tools Word processing software
Assistive Technology Services	Technology-Related Assistance for Individuals with Disabilities Act (TRAIDA, 1988)	Any service that directly assists an individual in the selection, acquisition, or use of an assistive technology device.	Training in using speech-to-text tools in the classroom

categorized. AT options include high-tech, mid-tech, and low-tech choices (Bouck, 2017).

◆ High-tech technology includes those tools and devices with more sophisticated technology (e.g., computers, tablets, print-reading software) and the apps or services for those devices (e.g., text-to-speech tools, virtual manipulatives).

◆ Mid-tech includes devices that generally work on battery power, the cost is lower, and the training need is low (e.g., smart pens).

◆ Low-tech includes AT tools that need less training and do not need power (e.g., checklists, pencil grips) (Bouck, 2017).

How do you obtain AT for your child? If your child has an IEP or 504 Plan and attends a public school, the AT will be provided if it is deemed necessary—meaning at no cost for you or your child to use at school. Your child can receive AT in the classroom through his or her IEP or 504 Plan. The selection and use of AT is a team-based approach. The remainder of this chapter breaks down the research on the use of AT for students with dysgraphia as well as the types of AT that many children use. Lastly, some resources for supporting AT in the home will be provided.

What the Research Reports

AT has truly changed the lives of people with disabilities, including those with dysgraphia, to support their access in both the home and school environments. Dictation apps and devices allow children to have their voices converted into written texts so they can communicate more quickly with their family and friends. With technology continuing to be more affordable, widely available, and used, the ability for your child to have their particular AT tool at their fingertips increases. AT such as word processing, speech recognition, text-to-speech tools, word prediction software, electronic dictionaries, and spell check have been used for decades to support students with learning disabilities in literacy (Bryant & Bryant, 2011; Ok et al., 2022). These AT tools can increase your child's ability across the writing process. For example, during prewriting, students can use an electronic graphic organizer; across the drafting phase they can use speech recognition to draft their essay; and in the editing and revision phase, they can use spell check and grammar check to support the accuracy of their essays (Bouck et al., 2015; Ok et al., 2022).

The area of handwriting and the transcription process of writing (transcription refers to the act of putting words on paper via handwriting or on the screen via typing) are areas in which AT has greatly assisted children with dysgraphia. Two tools, word processing and dictation, have been studied with students with learning disabilities. Word processing, or keyboarding, has been shown to have large positive effects on the errors that students make in their written essays (Graham & Perin, 2007; Perelmutter et al., 2017). By allowing students to type their responses, the quality of their output has been shown to increase. In addition to word processing, dictation tools, such as text-to-speech or scribing to an actual person, have also shown some positive effects (Gilespie & Graham, 2014). Last, speech recognition (SR) technology has been shown to be effective for students with LD. What is SR? SR is most commonly used in our everyday mobile devices and tablets. It is a technology in which the device recognizes a voice and then types the output. SR technology includes "Siri" on Apple devices, software (Dragon Naturally Speaking), and Google Chrome extensions (voice dictation). By using SR across the writing process, students have been found to increase the quality of their writing (Pennington et al., 2018).

Quick Start Guide to AT in Writing

With so many AT tools available, it can be overwhelming to select the best AT tool for your child. The selection of AT tools should be a *team-based approach*. You can request an IEP meeting to consider assistive technology, and it should have been considered at your child's first IEP meeting. In the IEP meeting, be informed and clear about what need you would like the AT to help your child with. Provide examples about the types of behaviors you are seeing at home (e.g., cannot write a sentence without support, has difficulty with the legibility of handwriting). Ask your child's teacher to describe the types of behavior they are seeing at school. Work with the IEP team to show your child's challenges occur at home and in school.

The SETT framework may help you. What is it? The SETT framework can be used to help the IEP team think about the best AT tool for your child. Table 8.2 describes each SETT component as well as some questions the team should ask in regard to choosing the best technology for your child.

TABLE 8.2 SETT Framework

Acronym	Defined
S=Student	**Student** Characteristics: • What are your child's strengths? • What are some areas of need? • How is your child doing academically in reading? Math? Writing? Daily activities?
E=Environment	Learning **Environment** • How is the classroom arranged? • What material is available?
T=Task	**Tasks** • What are the essential classroom tasks? • What are the expectations?
T=Tools	**Tools** • What technology tools should be considered? • High-, medium-, or low-tech?

Information from J. Zabala (2005)

Table 8.2 can help the IEP team process the choice of the best technology tools for your child. Next, the AT will be implemented with your child. Once in place, an IEP team member should collect data and information on the AT tool and if it benefits your child. The IEP team can always come back together to review the data and discuss how the tool is working. Talk with your child's special education teacher about how your child can use the AT at home. Note: your child can and should be able to use the AT across all of the school environments. If you have any unanswered questions, school districts usually have an AT specialist or an occupational therapist who can help provide guidance and expertise.

Think about even more technology that can help your child at home. There are a variety of educational tools that can be used to help support your child in practicing his or her writing skills at home. You can try these resources to determine if they help your child's writing. There are a variety of resources on the websites listed in Table 8.3, or you might even use YouTube for step-by-step instructions.

TABLE 8.3 Technology for the Writing Process

Stage	Tool	Description
Prewriting (Generating ideas, organizing)	Graphic Organizer: Word Mapping Software (e.g., Popplet: https://www.popplet.com/)	Electronic graphic organizers that help support students' writing
Drafting (Composing text)	Dictation tools: Siri Word prediction: Cowriter Softwarehttps://learningtools.donjohnston.com/ads/cowriter-trial/	This tool uses word prediction, among other features, to make sure your child doesn't get stuck on the spelling of a word
Editing (Checking spelling, grammar)	Grammarlyhttps://www.grammarly.com/	Spelling and grammar checking tool
Revising (Sentence structure, word choice)	Read & Write Softwarehttps://www.texthelp.com/products/read-and-write-education/	Read-aloud software can read the child's text aloud, which could help children hear their mistakes
Publishing (Completing final written product)	*VoiceThread*https://voicethread.com/	Use other publishing platforms to get your child engaged in the process

Summary

Choosing the right AT can be overwhelming. This chapter gave you information on the definition of AT as well as some pointers for how to best select AT for your child. Voice-to-text research showed that AT helps kids with dysgraphia. This knowledge can help you as you advocate for your child's needs with his or her teacher. The SETT framework provides good questions that can help support and guide the IEP team, with your input. It's clear that selecting and using appropriate technology can help make dysgraphia less frustrating for your child.

Resources

https://www.readingrockets.org/topics/assistive-technology/articles/
assistive-technology-writing AT for writing

https://www.atia.org/ Assistive Technology Industry Association

https://ceedar.education.ufl.edu/family-guide-to-at-home-learning/
Family Guide for At Home Learning

https://at3center.net/explore-at/ National Assistive Technology Center:
Provides assistance and links to your state.

https://www.pacer.org/ PACER: Center that provides a variety of assistance
and resources to families of children with disabilities. Search for AT
or any topic here

https://www.understood.org/articles/assistive-technology-what-it-is
-and-how-it-works What is AT?

References

Bouck, E. C. (2017). *Assistive technology.* Sage.

Bouck, E. C., Meyer, N. K., Satsangi, R., Savage, M. N., & Hunley, M. (2015).
Free computer-based assistive technology to support students
with high-incidence disabilities in the writing process. *Preventing
School Failure, 59*(2), 90–97. https://doi.org/10.1080/1045988X.2013
.841116

Bryant, D. P., & Bryant, B. R. (2011). *Assistive technology for people with
disabilities* (2nd ed.). Allyn & Bacon.

Gillespie, A., & Graham, S. (2014). A meta-analysis of writing interventions
for students with learning *Disabilities, 80*(4), 454–473. https://doi.org
/10.1177/0014402914527238

Graham, S., & Perin, D. (2007). A meta-analysis of writing instruction for
adolescent students. *Journal of Educational Psychology, 99,* 445–476.
https://doi.org/10.1037/0022-0663.99.3.44

Individuals with Disabilities Education Improvement Act of 2004, 20 U.S.C.
§ 614 et seq.

Ok, M. W., Rao, K., Pennington, J., & Ulloa, P. R. (2022). Speech recognition
technology for writing: Usage patterns and perceptions of
students with high incidence disabilities. *Journal of Special*

Education Technology, 37(2), 191–202.   https://doi.org/10.1177/0162643420979929

Pennington, J., Ok, M. W., & Rao, K. (2018). Beyond the keyboard: A review of speech recognition technology for supporting writing in schools. *International Journal for Educational Media and Technology, 12*(2), 47–55.

Perelmutter, B., McGregor, K. K., & Gordon, K. R. (2017). Assistive technology interventions for adolescents and adults with learning disabilities: An evidence-based systematic review and meta-analysis. *Computers & Education, 114*, 139–163. https://doi.org/10.1016/j.compedu.2017.06.005

Technology-Related Assistance for Individuals with Disabilities Act of 1988. Catalogue No. 850. (Senate Rpt. 100-438). Washington, DC: U.S. Government Printing Office.

Zabala, J. S. (2005). Using the SETT framework to level the learning field for students with disabilities. Retrieved August, 10, 2010.

9

Helping Teachers Understand and Accommodate for Dysgraphia

Helping Teachers Understand and Accommodate for Dysgraphia Explained

Max is an intelligent third-grade boy who has struggled with writing-related tasks since he started Kindergarten. Over the years, teachers would praise Max's talkative personality and creative storytelling but would also comment about his "messy writing," "lack of motivation," and "careless written work." Year after year, teachers suggested Max's parents work with him more in the home to encourage him to "slow down" and "take more pride" in his writing.

Max's mother Carmen was on it! She set up a fun writing corner for Max in the kitchen, purchased expensive handwriting practice workbooks from the internet, stocked up on pencils with his favorite comic characters on them, and gave him lots of fun novelty erasers. Carmen also sat with Max daily so she could make sure he did not "rush" through his work. She would often remind Max how unhappy his teachers would be to see such messy writing, knowing how eager he was to please them.

Despite her best efforts, Max's writing, and his attitude, only got worse from year to year. By third grade, Max was becoming tearful and even defiant at times. He started saying things like "this is stupid," or worse "I am stupid," during homework times. Carmen had never wanted to cause trouble with Max's teachers before this, but she was

DOI: 10.4324/9781003473879-9

beginning to suspect that there was more going on with Max than being just a "lazy or unmotivated writer." She was also frustrated that they were not doing more to help. She wondered… was he acting like this at school too?

Ms. Collier, Max's third-grade teacher, had seen some red flags early on when she welcomed him into her third-grade classroom this year. She could see how expressive Max was and didn't understand what was getting in the way of him writing as fluently as he spoke. It was like pulling teeth to get him to expand beyond the simplest sentence structure. He would erase so often, she sometimes wondered if he was just trying to "wait out" writing time, rather than trying to complete his work.

Ms. Collier consistently provided Max with rewards, praise, and encouragement to get him more excited about writing. She worked with him in small groups whenever possible. However, she was not seeing the progress she wanted to see and really believed he was capable of more. She also noticed that Max was beginning to shut down during writing tasks and had recently stopped handing in his homework… which was unlike the conscientious student she knew him to be. Having exhausted all of her usual tools to help struggling writers, Ms. Collier decided it was time to voice her escalating concerns for Max to her school specialists. She had begun to suspect that he may have a learning difference that required more than what she could give alone. She wondered: Are his parents having the same trouble one-on-one with him at home?

A Fresh Start

Like Carmen, you may find yourself at an uncomfortable crossroads, unsure of how to approach your child's teacher about your concerns without insinuating they are just not doing enough. Or, you may feel like things are not moving as quickly as they should be, given the concerns both you and your child's teacher have shared, and are not sure where to go from here without stepping on anyone's toes. Wherever you are in the educational journey, we want to ensure you have the information you need to move forward productively and confidently. The goal of this chapter is to empower you, not to put the responsibility of your child's school success on your shoulders alone! Rather, we want you to have the tools you may need to be an effective collaborator, communicator, and advocate within the school setting.

Just as importantly, we encourage you to let yourself "off the hook" for any doubts, guilt, frustration, or lack of understanding you may have in relation to your child's struggles prior to this diagnosis. Like Carmen, you may have been battling with your child at home, unsure at times if your child "could not" or just "would not" write. Like Max, the daily struggle may have become too much, and perhaps you too have stopped pushing homework completion, opting for a more peaceful afternoon with your child instead. Like Ms. Collier, your child's teachers may have shared the same concerns but could not yet "put their finger on" what was preventing him from putting his pencil to the paper. This is not uncommon: many dedicated parents and educators have shared the same lament… "if I only knew then, what I know now."

As discussed in Chapter 1, Dysgraphia is an "invisible disability." That is, you often don't know it exists, or the extent to which it will impact your child, until there is undeniable evidence showing your very capable child has fallen significantly behind his or her peers. Like Carmen and Ms. Collier, you and your child's teachers may also have been rewarding, praising, prompting, redirecting, and regretfully at times even admonishing your child's writing, thinking it was merely a "motivational deficit," rather than an inherent "skill deficit." In all fairness, with dysgraphia, it is often both. However, it is important to remember that none of us naturally gravitate toward the tasks that are hardest for us, and children with dysgraphia are no different. Writing difficulties, in particular, can invite avoidance behavior, as it can be laborious and, in the end, produce more visual evidence of what "they cannot do" for "all to see."

So, it is a good time to clear the slate for all involved. Prior to a comprehensive evaluation, it is very difficult to recognize when a child's lack of progress is the result of a specific learning disability requiring more focused intervention or just a lack of interest, experience, or quality instruction. This was true in the case of Max and, naturally, led to some frustration at home and at school before they had the support needed to come together as a team.

Claiming Your Seat at the Table

When the school contacted Carmen to notify her of their escalating concerns about the gaps in Max's academic achievement, she only remembered bits and pieces of the conversation... recalling terms like "evaluation" and "eligibility determination" during the quick conversation. Although Carmen was relieved she wasn't alone with her concerns, she was immediately overwhelmed by these discussions that were taking place about her son. She suddenly felt like everyone knew more about what was going on with her son than she did. Now she had more questions than answers, was unsure of what would happen next, and worried it would all just upset Max more.

As Carmen and Ms. Collier start to come together to better meet Max's needs, they will need to have a common language. They will also have to try to understand one another's unique perspective and expertise, so they can make collaborative and informed decisions together on Max's behalf. To help get Carmen and Ms. Collier on the same page, there are some key facts that Carmen, and all parents, will need to know about how school-based services work. Here, we will highlight some "must-know" facts to get you off to the right start or to help you get back on a forward-moving track so if you have lost your way.

Max Has Rights... and So Does Carmen

A federal law, the Individuals with Disabilities Education Act (IDEA), was first enacted in 1975 to protect the rights of students with disabilities enrolled in public schools. IDEA was reauthorized in 2004 outlining the following six guiding principles for public schools:

1. *Nondiscriminatory Evaluation*: Ensures all areas of concern are evaluated, including those brought forward by parents to determine if a child is eligible for special education services. The evaluation should be comprehensive enough to determine what academic and/or social support the child needs to be successful in the public school environment.
2. *Free, and Appropriate Public Education (FAPE)*: Ensures all children identified with a disability that impacts school success

receive an education that allows them to achieve meaningful goals free of charge to the family.

3. *Individualized Education Program (IEP)*: Ensures all eligible children receive individualized and specialized support and services to allow them to meet specific goals in the identified areas of need.

4. *Least Restrictive Environment (LRE)*: Ensures children with disabilities receive instruction in settings with their nondisabled peers to the greatest extent possible.

5. *Parent Participation*: Ensures parents have a right to know when their child is being evaluated in the school setting and grants them equal rights and participation throughout the special education process.

6. *Procedural Safeguards*: Ensures specific rights including parental consent prior to evaluation, parental access to all school records, and a process for settling any disputes. Schools are obligated to notify parents of these rights in their native language.

Special Education Services Are NOT Guaranteed for Max

Having a disability alone does not make your child eligible for special education services. Rather, there needs to be evidence that the deficits associated with the disability interfere with your child's achievement despite exposure to quality instruction. This provision is to protect your child from discrimination and to ensure your child receives the appropriate intensity of intervention, in the best setting, within the best timeline possible. Generally, you can expect the following process if your child has not yet been evaluated in an educational setting.

◆ *Referral/request for evaluation*: If a disability is suspected, your child's teacher will make a referral, or you will request a comprehensive evaluation based on your concerns.

◆ *Determining eligibility*: With your written consent, the educational team will assess all areas of concern to determine if your child is eligible for special education services under one or more of the 13 federally recognized categories (see resources for a full list of eligible categories and description). Whereas dysgraphia is recognized under the label of specific learning disability, it is helpful to know the eligibility categories that receive special education services in the case that your child presents with any co-occurring challenges.

◆ *Developing the Individualized Education Program (IEP)*: A meeting is scheduled to develop an IEP to guide future instruction. The IEP is developed by a collaborative team most commonly consisting of some or all of the following members in the case of dysgraphia:

◆ General education teacher: expert on the curriculum and your child's performance in the general education setting.

◆ Special education teacher: expert on specialized instruction and provision of special education services and supports across educational settings.

◆ School psychologist: expert on assessment and eligibility process.

◆ Occupational therapist: expert on handwriting and fine motor and related skills.

◆ Speech and language pathologist: expert on written expression and related skills.

◆ Administrator: expert on federal, district, and school policies and procedures.

◆ Parent: expert on the child's history and present struggles across settings.

◆ *Annual review/re-evaluation*: The IEP is reviewed/revised at a minimum once annually, and eligibility for services is re-evaluated at least every three years. A well-developed IEP will have <u>all</u> of the following components:

◆ Present levels of academic achievement and functional performance.

◆ Description of all educational services that will be provided.

◆ An explanation of the extent, if any, to which the child will not participate in the general education setting.

◆ Specific goals addressing each identified area of need.

◆ A transparent process for measuring and reporting progress toward the annual goals.
◆ Dates for the beginning of services and the frequency, location, and duration of the services that will be provided.
◆ Statement of the child's participation in district and state standardized assessments.

If Max Has an IEP, Carmen Needs to Be On the Lookout for SMART Goals

You cannot know if your child is making progress if you do not know what specifically they are working on and how it will be measured. The SMART acronym was developed to help educational teams ensure they have well-written goals with meaningful outcomes. Hedin and DeSpain (2018) described SMART goals as:

◆ Specific.
◆ Measurable.
◆ Action verbs.
◆ Realistic.
◆ Time-limited.

Example of a SMART goal for Max: Given a writing task, Max will independently utilize previously taught spelling strategies for 80% of unknown words on three out of four writing samples collected quarterly.

If Not Eligible for an IEP, Max Might Be Able to Be Supported by a 504 Plan

Section 504 of the Rehabilitation Act of 1973 is a civil rights law that prevents schools that receive federal funding from discriminating against students with disabilities. Section 504 provides protection for a wider range of impairments with less stringent criteria than THOSE required to meet eligibility under IDEA. Therefore, if your child does not qualify for an IEP, a 504 may still be a possibility. Under 504, it must be documented that your child has a disability, mental or physical, that limits one or more life activities: in this case, writing. With documentation, a plan will be developed to determine what accommodations and supports your child will need and who will deliver and monitor these services. The main points to remember about IEPs and 504s that need to be included here are:

♦ Both acknowledge a disability.
♦ Both are offered free of charge to families.
♦ Both include the parent as an active team member.
♦ Both provide a list of accommodations/supports to address learning barriers.
♦ Only an IEP provides individualized learning goals and desired outcomes.
♦ Only an IEP provides specialized instruction with designated times and settings.
♦ 504 Plans are always implemented in the general education classroom.

There Is a Difference between Accommodations and Modifications

Accommodations are designed to help your child overcome barriers. They should NOT change the curriculum that your child learns or lower expectations for performance. Modifications, on the other hand, allow for adaptations to the curriculum to better meet the ability level of the child and to set more appropriate learning outcomes. The goal is to only provide the level of assistance a child needs while maintaining the highest level of independence and rigor appropriate for each child.

There Are Different Ways Max's Learning Differences Can Be Accommodated

♦ Timing/scheduling can be adapted (when and for how long work is done).
♦ Setting/environment can be adapted (where work is completed).
♦ Response expectations can be adapted (how work is shown).
♦ Presentation of subject matter can be adapted (how instruction/materials are presented).

There Are Some Common Accommodations for Dysgraphia That Carmen Should Know About

Accommodations can be a mix of high (e.g., text-to-speech software) and low technology (e.g., pencil grips). Although there are a number of wonderful advanced technological tools to help struggling writers, it is important that your child and those who support them can use them consistently and comfortably across settings. Not all will work for everyone, and your child will be the expert on what works best in the long run. For now, it is helpful to know a variety of interventions that work for many children with dysgraphia so you know what tools may need to be added to your child's toolbox over time.

+ Pencil grips.
+ Specialized paper for writing.
+ Graph paper for math problems.
+ Typed outlines of lessons.
+ Use of a slant board.
+ Extra time on tests.
+ Preferential seating.
+ Note taker or scribe.
+ Recorded instructions/lectures.
+ Oral presentation of work.
+ Use of keyboard/computer.
+ Assistive technology (Word prediction software, talk-to-text software).
+ Graphic organizers.
+ Handouts vs. copying from the board.
+ Breaking assignments into smaller steps.
+ Providing models for writing expectations.

There Is Such a Thing as Too Many Accommodations!

There is a tendency to think more is better. You want to be comprehensive in listing the supports needed but do not want the outcome to be generic lists of accommodations no one can remember, understand or know how to do. Whether they are provided in an IEP or in a 504 Plan, accommodations should always be:

- ◆ Individualized.
- ◆ Setting appropriate.
- ◆ Age appropriate.
- ◆ Evidence-based.

It is important to note that accommodations are designed to help your child overcome barriers. They should NOT change the curriculum that your child learns or lower expectations for performance. The goal is to only provide the level of assistance a child needs while maintaining the highest level of independence and academic rigor appropriate for your child.

Finding Your Voice

Carmen slowly but surely began to speak out and make requests more confidently during that third-grade year. In the beginning, she felt "outnumbered" by professionals at meetings, so she would bring her sister with her for support. Her sister would help her remember the important questions she wanted to ask and would take some notes for her so she could be present at the meeting, yet have something to reference and check in with later.

Carmen also found some great resources through other parents she had met after Max was found eligible for special education services for a specific learning disability in writing. These helped her communicate clearly about her son and keep them all accountable to the established timelines with the help of some simple record-keeping. Having a team of support at school and at home made all the difference for Max and for Carmen, and we trust the same will be true for you.

What the Research Reports

Indicators of High-Quality Collaboration

Decades and decades of educational research emphasize the essential role collaboration plays in the success of students with and without disabilities (Shamberger & Friend, 2013). Defined in the simplest terms possible, collaboration occurs when all members of an inclusive community (including parents) work together as equals in order to effectively meet the needs of shared students. Although each member of the team may bring different expertise, all have a shared goal—to produce meaningful outcomes for the students they serve. A convergence of professional literature focused on collaboration in inclusive school settings has identified a few defining characteristics for effective collaboration that you should keep in mind (Cook & Friend, 2010)

♦ Collaboration must be voluntary.
♦ Collaborators must have parity (equality).
♦ Collaborators must have shared decision-making power.
♦ Collaborators must have shared goals.
♦ Collaborators must share resources.
♦ Collaborators must share accountability.

Common Obstacles to Collaboration

Despite the legal and long-standing support for collaboration to improve outcomes for students with disabilities, educators and parents alike may encounter a number of barriers that prevent effective collaboration from being realized as quickly as desired. Knowing these will help you identify these common roadblocks and support troubleshooting as a team to avoid getting "stuck" behind one or more of these for too long.

♦ A lack of time.
♦ Equal access to resources.
♦ Different communication styles.
♦ Personality conflicts.
♦ Fear of losing control/autonomy.
♦ Fear of being judged.
♦ Absence of training.
♦ Absence of support from school or district leaders.

Recommendations for Educators Working with Parents

In 2020, Salone and colleagues published a list of research-based recommendations for creating a more collaborative culture in public schools across the United States. In their review, they acknowledged that many parents report feeling uncomfortable in educational settings and are made to feel like their participation in educational decision-making is unwanted. In order to provide better guidance to educators in support of parents, this group of researchers compiled a list of simple yet essential best practices summarized below (Solone et al., 2020).

- ◆ Promote communication (quality vs. quantity, timely, avoid jargon, open and honest, etc.).
- ◆ Promote equity (acknowledge family as experts, admit when you don't have an answer etc.).
- ◆ Promote trust (be reliable, show concern etc.).
- ◆ Promote respect (honor ethnicity, language, culture, know family commitments, be on time, etc.).

Recommendations for Parents Working with Educators

The old adage "communication is a two-way street" remains true here. Although the onus to establish a collaborative culture with parents lies with the school professionals as mandated by federal legislation, they can only work with you if you are willing to work with them. Understanding the need for additional guidance for parents, The Center for Appropriate Dispute Resolution in Special Education (CADRE) produced a document titled "Parents Perceptions on the IEP Process: Considerations for Improved Practice" (Reiman et al., 2010). Among the comprehensive recommendations made there for all stakeholders, the authors summarized the research informing best practices for parents to fulfill their important role effectively (Fish, 2008). Specifically, they directed parents to:

- ◆ Become knowledgeable about special education law and the parameters of the IEP process.
- ◆ Take the initiative to educate themselves about special education issues.
- ◆ Be persistent in requesting needed services for their children.

- Prepare before IEP meetings by educating themselves about special laws and processes.
- Speak up during meetings.
- Be unafraid to ask questions and make suggestions.

Quick Start Guide to Helping Teachers Understand and Accommodate for Dysgraphia

Communicate and Collaborate

We began this chapter by introducing you to Max, his mother, and his teacher to illustrate how each may have a different perspective, but they all have one thing in common—they are doing their best but need more help! Carmen recognized missed opportunities to communicate her concerns to Max's teachers earlier because she did not want to "cause trouble." Carmen is not alone in her hesitance to reach out. Often parents are afraid to "challenge them" or "step on any toes." Other parents are fearful their child will be stigmatized or discriminated against if a learning difference is brought to light in the classroom. Some feel embarrassed... thinking they are failing at parenting when their efforts fall short or their child starts to misbehave or speak poorly about themselves. These are thought traps that you will want to avoid in order to move forward with confidence. The laws protect you and your child, and any information about your child that can be gathered and shared will be beneficial.

Carmen invested a lot of time and money helping her child over the years and should be commended for her efforts. Making writing more fun and motivating is always a good thing and we recommend it (see Chapter 7 for more on this). However, Carmen also needed the help of trained professionals to identify and intervene on the core deficits of dysgraphia that manifested with more intensity as Max got older and writing expectations increased.

Keep in mind you are not expected to be an expert on all things school-related. Nor do you need to feel intimidated by experts, as you will always be the consummate expert on your own child. If you have questions, ask. If a conversation is moving too quickly, set a slower pace. If you are concerned about your child's progress, ask for data or work samples to get a better "picture" of where they are at and where they need to be. If you are not sure if your child is getting accommodations consistently, ask when they are accessed and how well each is working. Ask your child what is accessible daily, help your child understand the purpose of their own accommodations, and let them inform you of their own preferences.

Keep in mind that it may not always be evident to you the progress being made in the school setting, just as it may not be evident to the school what struggles you are having in the home. So, if you are hesitating to reach out about your concerns, at any time along this journey, don't! Reach out sooner than later. When you do be sure to:

- ◆ Communicate in writing when possible.
- ◆ Communicate in the preferred mode/time articulated by the teacher (e.g., email vs. phone, morning vs. evening).
- ◆ Communicate with a positive and respectful, yet assertive tone.
- ◆ Communicate concerns with data, samples, and examples, whenever possible.

Consider keeping a written record of your communications with the school. Having organized records can help you stay on top of required timelines and ensure you and the school team are maintaining reciprocal and timely communication. Your record-keeping can be as low- or high-tech as you are comfortable with (notebook, phone app, etc.). Choose one that can be completed with ease and is sustainable for you. There are a number of downloadable templates and electronic tools available for this purpose. A link to a resource describing various home-school communication tools is provided in the reference section at the end of this chapter. Below is an example of Carmen's preferred communication tool.

COMMUNICATION LOG

Date: _____

Time:_____

Person(s) Communicated with: _____

Form of Contact:_____

Summary of Conversation/Meeting/Contact: _____

Follow-up Requested:_____

FIGURE 9.1 Communication Tool

Some parents also choose to create quick reference documents such as "accommodations at a glance forms" or "student summary sheets." While being mindful of their child's confidentiality, parents may opt to share these "cheat sheets" with all trusted adults working with their child. Parents report this as being a useful tool to give to a new team of teachers at the beginning of the school year or to share with private tutors and service providers who work with their child outside of the school setting.

Example of Carmen's "Accommodations at a Glance" Sheet for Max

My Name: *My Grade:*   *My Teacher:*

During Instructions I need: _____

During Tests I need: _____

Assistive Technology I can use on my own: _____

I am Positively Reinforced by:

During Independent Work I need:

During Partner Work I need:

Notes:

FIGURE 9.2 Quick Reference Document

These documents are not meant to replace the more comprehensive documents by any means. Rather, they serve as a quick reference and visual reminder of the must-know facts related to the child's success in these environments.

Ask and Advocate

In this chapter, we explain what Carmen, and all parents, should know to navigate school-based services effectively and comfortably. We emphasize effective communication and respectful collaboration with schools. However, good collaboration does not mean everyone agrees all the time. We also acknowledge that procedures are not always followed with 100% compliance, 100% of the time, in 100% of settings. For this reason, we encourage you to keep the following rights first and foremost in mind and proceed accordingly:

◆ If you suspect a disability is the inherent cause of the writing impairments at any time, you can request (in writing!) that an educational evaluation be initiated for your child. When a written request is made and parent consent is obtained, public schools are mandated to comply within a specified timeline.

◆ Your written consent is required before your child can be evaluated to determine eligibility for special education services in the school setting.

◆ You have access to all of your child's school records.

◆ You must be notified in a timely manner about official meetings that will take place about your child during the eligibility and IEP process.

◆ You have the right to bring anyone you need to support your child's IEP meeting.

◆ If you believe your child's evaluation has been unfair or biased in some way, you have the right to request an Independent Educational Evaluation (IEE) be administered by a neutral third party.

◆ If your child is on an IEP, you should be notified of your child's progress toward their goals at least as often as parents of children without disabilities are notified of progress (i.e., standard report card schedule).

◆ If your child is on an IEP, you can request an interim meeting if you are concerned about a lack of progress: meeting annually is the minimum, not the maximum.

◆ Federal laws mandate that educational decisions must be data-driven. Programmatic decisions are not made based on hunches or gut feelings. You can request the data that informs the decisions being made about your child. You can also ask questions if any document or educational jargon is unclear to you.

Although this is not an exhaustive list, knowing you are an equal and valued member of your child's educational team and knowing there are laws that protect you and your child is essential for becoming a confident and lifelong advocate. At the end of this chapter, we provide a number of resources for you to reference for more comprehensive information about the laws, procedures, and recommendations described throughout this chapter.

Summary

Here, we provide you with the basic facts you may need to navigate school-based services more confidently. By sharing Carmen's story with you, we hope you can feel part of a shared community and avoid the same pitfalls and mindsets that prevented her from being a confident and effective member of her child's educational team from the beginning.

You are already the expert on your child. By providing key indicators of respectful collaborative relationships and a framework for evaluating the quality of the accommodations and supports recommended for your child, we hope to empower you to be a firm and knowledgeable advocate and encourage you to claim your seat at the table and find your voice so you can proceed with confidence from here.

Resources

IRIS | IEPs: Developing High-Quality Individualized Education Programs (vanderbilt.edu) IRIS Module Describing Components of an IEP

10 Basics of the Special Education Process under IDEA (parentcenterhub .org) The Individuals with Disabilities Education Act Guidelines for Special Education Services

Protecting Students With Disabilities (ed.gov) US Department of Education Office for Civil Rights

20 Parent Communication Log Templates | Free Parent-Teacher Daily Communication Sheets (adayinourshoes.com) Examples of Home-School Communication Tools

References

Cook, L., & Friend, M. (2010). The state of the art of collaboration on behalf of students with disabilities. *Journal of Educational and Psychological Consultation, 20*(1), 1–8.

Fish, W. W. (2008). The IEP meeting: Perceptions of parents of students who receive special education services. *Preventing School Failure, 53*(1), 8–14.

Hedin, L., & DeSpain, S. (2018). SMART or not? Writing specific, measurable IEP goals. *Teaching Exceptional Children, 51*(2), 100–110. https://doi .org/10.1177/0040059918802587

Solone, C. J., Thornton, B. E., Chiappe, J. C., Perez, C., Rearick, M. K., & Falvey, M. A. (2020). Creating collaborative schools in the United States: A review of best practices. *International Electronic Journal of Elementary Education, 12*(3), 283–292.

Shamberger, C. T., & Friend, M. (2013). Working together for learning together: Supporting students and teachers with collaborative instruction. *Journal of the American Academy of Special Education Professionals, 119*, 133.

10

Dysgraphia

Your Child's Self-Esteem and Mindset

Dysgraphia and Your Child's Self-Esteem and Mindset Explained

"I hate writing," was a frequent comment from one author's child. "It's stupid and it hurts my brain," was another classic comment. Unfortunately, these quotes capture the sentiment of many children with dysgraphia. Writing is a labor-intensive, time-consuming, brain-draining activity. However, as a parent, it is easy to think your child is just being lazy or unmotivated to write. You might think to yourself, "Suck it up buttercup. Everyone has to write." But when it's dysgraphia, it's much more than your child simply being lazy.

As you've read throughout this book, dysgraphia is a true *hidden* learning disability that *substantially* interferes with your child's writing. It is a hidden or invisible learning disability because your child's outward appearance looks perfect: but dysgraphia is there within their internal wiring. Now consider the word, substantially. It means in a strong manner or to a great extent. This is the point you must help other adults understand. Having dysgraphia is a big deal. Your child's writing is hindered to a great extent because consider what it takes for your child to write. Many cognitive systems contribute to writing including:

DOI: 10.4324/9781003473879-10

- ◆ Memory.
- ◆ Sustained attention.
- ◆ Processing speed.
- ◆ Language.
- ◆ Motor.
- ◆ Vision.
- ◆ Planning.
- ◆ Organizing.
- ◆ Critical thinking.
- ◆ Self-monitoring.
- ◆ Spelling.
- ◆ Grammar.

Given all the systems that must simultaneously work together, it's no wonder that many children struggle with their written expression. Writing problems often occur when one or more of these systems don't function well.

As your child progresses through the early elementary grades, writing instruction emphasizes the mechanics of writing, but by the fourth grade, the focus changes to writing longer pieces emphasizing content and creative thinking. If your child's writing mechanics have not become automatic processes, they will have fewer mental resources to think creatively because they remain bogged down in the mechanics. This is why many children with dysgraphia speak better than they write since verbal words flow easier than written words.

Your child's self-esteem can be affected by repeated failures with written expression. Self-esteem (also known as self-concept) is a broad term used to describe the way we view ourselves and feel about our abilities. There is our global self-esteem as well as area-specific areas of self-esteem such as academic self-esteem, athletic self-esteem, musical self-esteem, physical appearance self-esteem, and social self-esteem. Consider yourself. You might believe you have good overall self-esteem but lower self-esteem in a specific area such as athletic self-esteem. Your child might have voiced lower academic self-esteem by telling you, "I'm good in math but not good at reading, writing, and spelling." Children have self-awareness and know they struggle in writing. We can improve any area of our self-esteem, but it takes many small successes that accumulate and contribute to our overall belief. George Bear and colleagues (2002) conducted a meta-analysis of the research analyzing 61 studies of the self-concept of students with learning disabilities (LD) as compared to students without. Their results were encouraging and supported no significant difference in the global self-concept of students with learning disabilities as compared to their peers. However, students with learning disabilities had lower academic self-concepts. They wrote, "This study supported the conclusion that the self-concept of students with LD is fairly similar to their non-LD peers in all areas but intellectual/academics" (p. 423).

In addition to self-esteem, your child's mindset also affects how they view and approach writing. In today's schools, there is often talk about how students must develop a "growth" mindset, which is the belief that an attribute such as intelligence or academic performance is changeable. We can improve our ability, behavior, and attributes, and have resiliency after a setback. On the contrary, a fixed mindset is the belief that our attributes are unchangeable or in other words, "We got what we got." When it comes to writing, a child with a growth mindset is more likely to say, "I'm not a great writer, *yet*." A child with a fixed mindset says, "I'm not a good writer," and believes they never will be. This creates feelings of disengagement and helplessness which certainly don't help your child's writing.

What the Research Reports

Poor handwriting is often defined by handwriting legibility and slow performance time or handwriting speed (Feder & Manjnemer, 2007; Rosenblum et al., 2003). Thus, children with dysgraphia require more time to complete classroom-based handwriting assignments. Furthermore, Engle-Yeger noted, "Children with dysgraphia erase more, complain about hand pain, and are unwilling to write and do their homework" (p. 183).

Thus, children who struggle with writing find it difficult to keep up with any written assignments. This also affects written homework assignments (Racine et al., 2008).

Feder and Majnemer (2007) explained it succinctly when they wrote, "The development of writing ability is not only important in building a child's self-esteem, but is considered an essential ingredient for success in school" (p. 312). This is especially true, as Engle-Yeger and colleagues (2009) noted that handwriting is a central occupation of school-age children. Regardless of academic subject, school requires a tremendous amount of written output.

There are at least two main reasons why handwriting difficulties interfere with a child's academic achievement. First, children who don't master the mechanical aspects of handwriting do not have the higher-order processes needed for text composition. Second, teachers often give better grades for neatly written papers as compared to papers with messy and illegible handwriting (Graham et al., 1998; Santangelo & Graham, 2016).

Engle-Yeger and colleagues (2009) researched the self-efficacy (a person's belief in their ability to complete a task) of children with dysgraphia and reported "that children with dysgraphia who exhibited lower self-efficacy regarding handwriting abilities indeed had impaired handwriting processes and products, as manifested in impaired fluency and spatial arrangement and slower handwriting velocity" (p.189). They went on to explain that children with dysgraphia have difficulty organizing their writing and make more corrections, which results in them spending a longer time writing.

They also noted that children with dysgraphia used inappropriate spacing between letters or words, incorrect letter shapes, and letter inversions, and mixed up different letter forms, all making handwriting tasks longer and contributing to less automatic handwriting. They concluded, "When a child with dysgraphia compares his or her performance to that of typical peers in the class, it may negatively affect his or her sense of self-efficacy regarding handwriting performance" (p. 189).

Professor Frank Pajares (2003) wrote, "Students' writing confidence and competence increase when they are provided with process goals (i.e., specific strategies they can use to improve their writing) and regular feedback regarding how well they are using such strategies" (p. 147). He also explained that self-concept differs from self-efficacy because self-concept also includes perceptions of one's self-worth. Interestingly, his research supported gender differences in written expression and that "It is evident that, regardless of the ratings that boys and girls provide on writing self-efficacy measures, girls consider themselves better writers than the boys" (p. 149).

Not surprisingly, if your child struggles in reading, he or she is also likely to struggle in writing. Graham and colleagues (2021) wrote,

> Children who experience difficulty decoding words, reading text fluently, or comprehending and critically evaluating text are at a disadvantage when writing. Such problems make it more likely they will misinterpret writing directions, experience difficulty obtaining information from source materials, or create less cogent and polished compositions.
>
> (Graham and colleagues (2021),
> p. 1483)

Reading helps support your child's writing in that they need to read and follow the assignment directions. Reading is also needed during writing when your child must research content to include in their writing. Your child must also rely upon his or her reading to read and reread their written text to ensure it makes sense and proof for any problems.

The research is quite clear that children with dysgraphia take longer to complete written tasks, have less legible penmanship, have difficulty with the mechanics of writing, and boys have lower self-efficacy when writing than girls. These challenges often create a child's negative attitude toward writing.

Quick Start Guide to Enhancing Self-Esteem and Mindset

Your words matter. You play an important role in developing your child's academic self-esteem. As Frank Pajares (2003) noted,

> As children strive to exercise control over their surroundings, their first transactions are mediated by adults who can either empower them with self-assurance or diminish their fledgling self-beliefs. Young children are not proficient at making accurate self-appraisals, and so they must rely on the judgments of others to create their own judgments of confidence and of self-worth.
>
> (Frank Pajares (2003), p. 153)

Use encouraging and avoid discouraging remarks about your child's writing. Your child might have the worst-looking handwriting you've seen, but think it and don't say it. Samantha put it well when she said, "My fourth grade son's handwriting looks like a kindergarten student's work but I tell him it's all about the effort, not how it looks. His dad has a harder time doing that." We also encourage you to emphasize that the process of creating good content is more important than its appearance. Typing and voice-to-text accommodations can help polish up your child's messy handwriting.

Mold your child's mindset. Everyone talks. We are usually talking out loud with someone or talking to ourselves. When we talk in our mind this is called self-talk, or inner-voice, or inner speech. Self-talk is important because it is how we think about, conceptualize, and solve many of our daily problems. It shapes our mindset, so it is important to teach your child to develop positive self-talk because it is related to our self-esteem. If our self-talk is mostly negative, then we start to believe it and feel negative about ourselves. Positive self-talk leads to positive actions. How many times a day do you say positive versus negative thoughts to yourself?

Think about your child and school. Does your child say positive statements such as: "School is OK. I'll give it my best shot." Or "I can do well on this quiz because I studied." If your child is not using positive self-talk, then she is less likely to perform well in school or in other areas of life such as playing sports. One author used an analogy like this with his son when he was thinking negatively. He said to his son,

> When you get up to bat in baseball do you tell yourself you'll strike out or get a hit? Right, you tell yourself you'll get a hit. So, when you are doing your homework are you telling yourself you can try to get it done or that you just hate homework?

Then they discuss how he could perform better with a positive mindset and thought process.

As parents, we can show our children how we use positive self-talk during everyday events. The next time you are preparing for an event such as a job interview, client presentation, sports event, or trying on a pair of jeans, explain your thoughts. Give your child some insight into your thinking by talking about your thoughts aloud. Teach your child to believe in him or herself to mold their growth mindset so they can continue to learn and perform better in school and life.

Build writing success. Be sure to refer back to Chapter 7 about Making Writing Fun, as developing strengths in children is a process. If it's not currently writing, what does your child excel at? As a child, Jim grew up in the Evel Knievel era, and he was the best kid in his Miami neighborhood at jumping a bicycle across two open ramps, and he has the scars to prove it. Of course, his parents did not see this as his natural affinity and encouraged him to become a dentist. Jim had a negative mindset and self-efficacy toward math and science and did not pursue this career. However, in hindsight, he could have become a dentist if his parents had just kept encouraging him that he had what it took but that he just needed to keep working at it. At ten years old, his lack of math and science self-efficacy shaped his future career.

We tell you this because you know your child best, and you might need to continue to nudge and believe for your child until he or she develops the self-efficacy belief on their own. You can help your child obtain the goal of becoming an adequate writer.

Since writing is one main occupation for kids, and is a skill, it can be developed. Work to improve your child's writing, but simultaneously build their other natural talents, as it's these talents that will often shape college major or career choices.

Building your child's writing requires intentionality, and sometimes parents must apply caution not to just do the writing for the child because it is easier. When your child has dysgraphia, understanding, support, and accommodations are needed: but not a free pass. Dysgraphia testing (as described in Chapter 2) often provides you with the paperwork containing accommodations (as described in Chapter 9) you can make for your child. You can then implement voice-to-text technology, spell or grammar check, or scribe for your child. Your child provides the creative thinking, and his or her accommodations help support the mechanics of their writing.

Here are three ways to build your child's strengths. First, allow your child to choose the topic to write about. We write more and better when we have an interest in what we are writing. Allow him to write a comic, graphic novel, lyrics to a favorite movie or song. Texting a relative is writing, and texting or writing down preferred items for your grocery list is writing. Second, don't give up on your child. You might invest time and money into your child's therapies only to see minimal progress. Don't worry, as it's a building block experience that helps shape him or her. Finally, teach keyboarding. One of Jim's most valuable middle school classes was taking a typing class, but many schools don't formally teach keyboarding anymore. This year you can give your child a life skill that is crucial in today's world. Use Type to Learn, Mavis Beacon, or other keyboarding programs and require your child to complete 10–15 minutes per day of keyboard training. Going forward, typing proficiency can help make your child's life easier.

Summary

Your child's writing self-concept (the way we view ourselves and feel about our abilities) and self-efficacy (a person's belief in their ability to complete a task) might be below expected levels. Nevertheless, your child can develop a "growth" mindset, which is the belief that an attribute such as intelligence or academic performance is changeable. You can teach your child that we can improve our ability, behavior, and attributes, and have resiliency after a setback. On the contrary, a fixed mindset is the belief that our attributes are unchangeable. As a parent, your words of encouragement or discouragement help shape your child's belief about writing and their global self-esteem. Speak to your child about what you want him or her to become, such as "Your hard work will pay off. You completed X number of assignments this quarter. You have what it takes." You can create small opportunities for writing success including researching and writing on your child's strengths, continuing occupational or other therapies, and helping your child become a skilled typist.

Resources

https://www.handwritingsolutions.org: They offer individual handwriting tutoring

www.Scribblitt.com: Teachers might use Scribblitt.com to create a student publishing program in their classroom

https://pathwaysforlearning.com/grotto-grip/: A pencil grip designed by an OT to reduce hand fatigue and pencil pressure

https://pathwaysforlearning.com/redispace/: Redi Space writing paper to help with spacing and alignment

References

Bear, G. G., Minke, K. M., & Manning, M. A. (2002). Self-concept of students with learning disabilities: A meta-analysis. *School Psychology Review*, *31*(3), 405–427.

Engel-Yeger, B., Nagauker-Yanuv, L., & Rosenblum, S. (2009). Handwriting performance, self-reports, and perceived self-efficacy among children with dysgraphia. *The American Journal of Occupational Therapy*, *63*(2), 182–192.

Graham, S., Aitken, A. A., Hebert, M., Camping, A., Santangelo, T., Harris, K. R., ... Ng, C. (2021). Do children with reading difficulties experience writing difficulties? A meta-analysis. *Journal of Educational Psychology, 113*(8), 1481.

Graham, S., Berninger, V., Weintraub, N., & Schafer, W. (1998). Development of handwriting speed and legibility in Grades 1–9. *The Journal of Educational Research, 92*(1), 42–52.

Feder, K. P., & Majnemer, A. (2007). Handwriting development, competency, and intervention. *Developmental Medicine & Child Neurology, 49*(4), 312–317.

Pajares, F. (2003). Self-efficacy beliefs, motivation, and achievement in writing: A review of the literature. *Reading & Writing Quarterly, 19*(2), 139–158.

Racine, M. B., Majnemer, A., Shevell, M., & Snider, L. (2008). Handwriting performance in children with attention deficit hyperactivity disorder (ADHD). *Journal of Child Neurology, 23*(4), 399–406.

Rosenblum, S., Weiss, P. L., & Parush, S. (2003). Product and process evaluation of handwriting difficulties. *Educational Psychology Review, 15*, 41–81.

Santangelo, T., & Graham, S. (2016). A comprehensive meta-analysis of handwriting instruction. *Educational Psychology Review, 28*, 225–265.

Printed in the United States
by Baker & Taylor Publisher Services